Lesson 1: Getting Started

To crochet, you need only a steel crochet hook, some crochet thread and a tapestry needle.

Hooks

If you've not worked with steel hooks before, you may at first feel clumsy and awkward. For an experienced crocheter, this is a bit of a surprise, suddenly feeling all thumbs again just as when you first learned to crochet. But this will pass in a few hours of crocheting, as you adjust your tension and working methods to the new tool. Soon you'll be working much more by feel than when using heavier yarns and aluminum hooks.

Steel hooks come in many sizes, from very fine steel hooks used to make intricate doilies and lace, to great big fat ones of plastic or wood used to make bulky sweaters or rugs.

The hooks you will use most often are made of steel, are about 5" long, which is shorter than the aluminum or plastic hook. Steel hooks are sized numerically from 14 (the smallest) to 0 (the largest). For our lessons, you'll need a size 7 hook, a medium size.

The steel crochet hook looks like this:

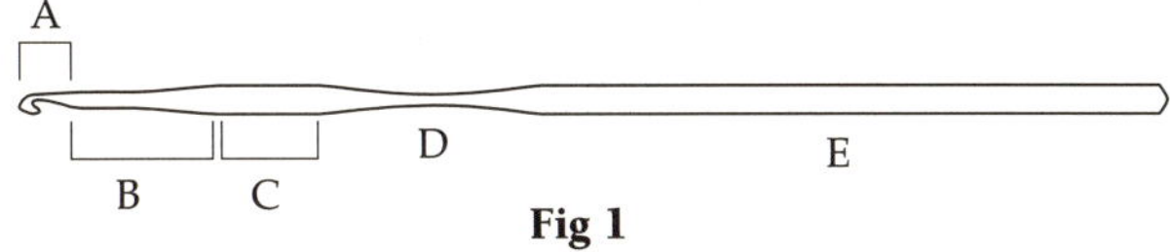

Fig 1

In **Fig 1**, (A) is the hook end, which is used to hook the thread and draw it through other loops of thread (called stitches). (B) is the throat, a shaped area that helps you slide the stitch up onto (C) the working area. (D) is the fingerhold, a flattened area that helps you grip the hook comfortably, usually with your thumb and third finger; and (E) is the handle, which rests under your fourth and little fingers, and provides balance for easy, smooth work.

It is important that every stitch is made on the working area, never on the throat (which would make the stitch too tight) and never on the fingergrip (which would stretch the stitch). If you are having difficulty with this, put a piece of cellophane tape around the hook to keep the stitches from sliding past the correct area. With practice, you'll work in the right place automatically.

The hook is held in the right hand, with the thumb and third finger on the fingergrip, and the index finger near the tip of the hook (**Fig 2**).

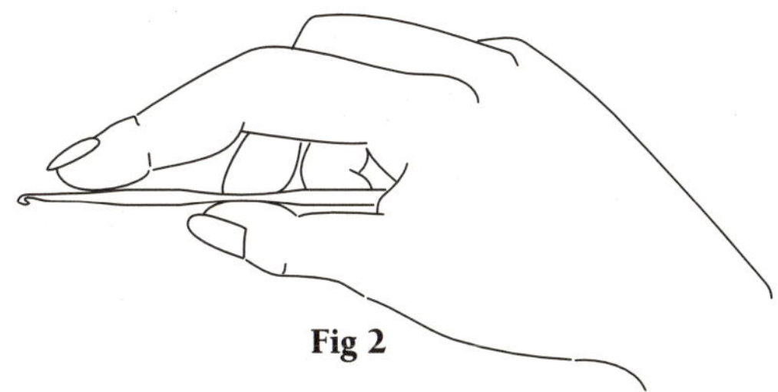

Fig 2

The hook should be turned slightly toward you, not facing up or down. **Fig 3** shows how the hook is held, viewing from underneath the hand. The hook should be held firmly, but not tightly.

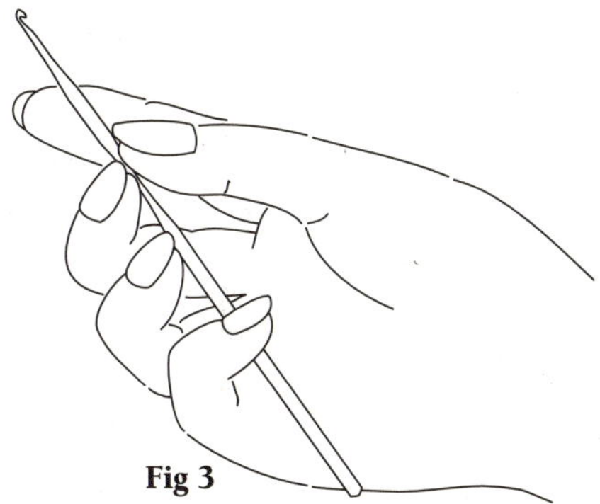

Fig 3

Thread

Thread comes in many sizes: from very fine crochet cotton used for lace making and tatting, to sizes 30, 20, and 10 used for doilies and bedspreads. The larger the number, the thinner the thread. The most commonly used thread is size 10, and is often called bedspread-weight. It is readily available in white, ecru, and cream as well as a wide variety of beautiful colors. This is the weight we will use in our lessons. Always read thread labels carefully. The label will tell you how much thread is in the ball, in ounces, grams, meters or yards; the type of thread, usually cotton, and its washability. Also, there is usually a dye lot number. This number assures you that the color of each ball with this number is the same. The same color may vary from dye lot to dye lot creating variations in color when a project is completed. Therefore, when purchasing thread for a project, it is important to match the dye lot number on the balls and purchase enough thread to complete the project.

You'll need a blunt-pointed sewing needle with an eye big enough to carry the thread for weaving in thread ends and sewing seams. This is a size 18 steel tapestry needle.

Lesson 2: Chain Stitch (abbreviated ch)

Crochet usually begins with a series of chain stitches called a beginning or starting chain. Begin by making a slip knot on the hook about 4" from the thread end. Loop the thread as in **Fig 4**.

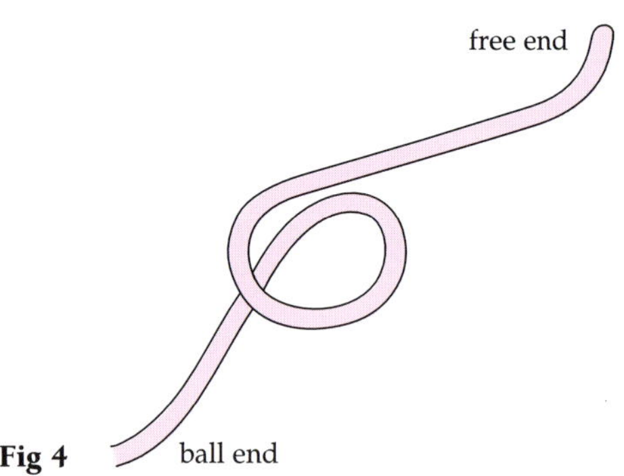

Fig 4

Insert hook through center of loop and hook the free end (**Fig 5**).

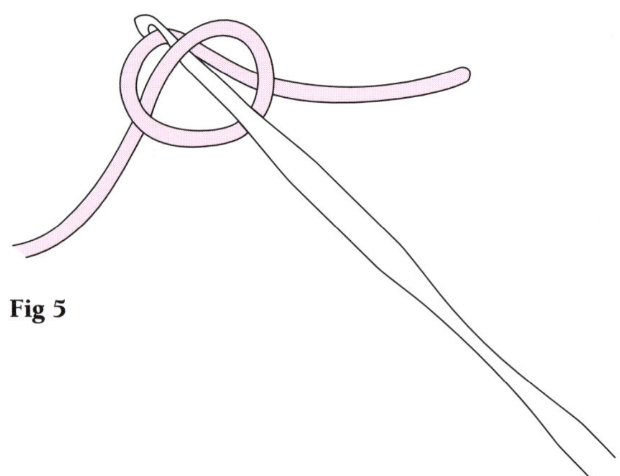

Fig 5

Pull this through and up onto the working area of the hook (**Fig 6**).

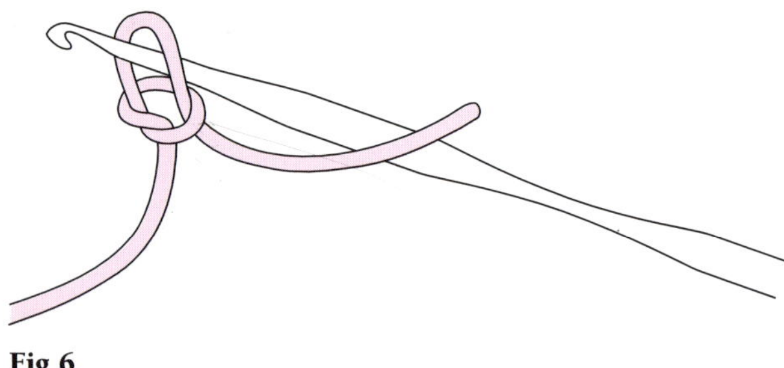

Fig 6

Pull thread end to tighten the loop (**Fig 7**).

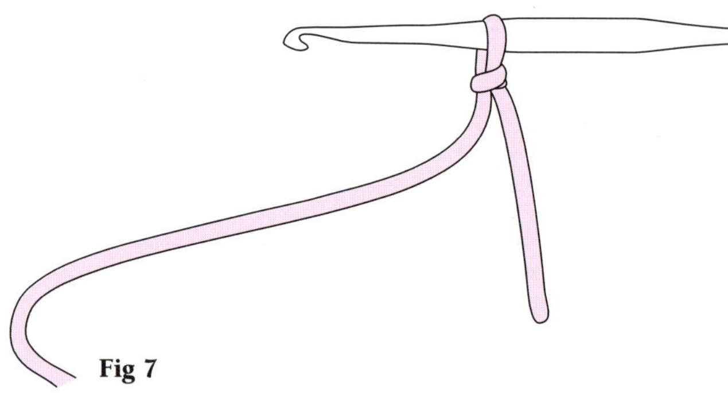

Fig 7

It should be firm, but loose enough to slide back and forth easily on the hook. Be sure you still have about a 4" thread end.

Hold the hook, now with its slip knot, in your right hand (**Fig 8**).

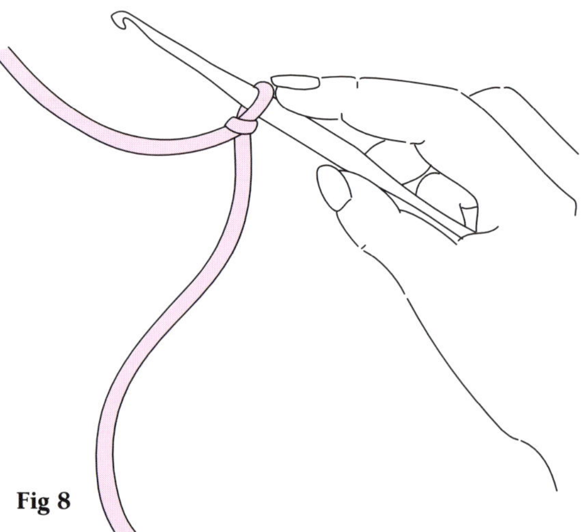

Fig 8

Now let's make the first chain stitch.

Step 1: Hold the base of the slip knot with the thumb and index finger of your left hand, and thread from the ball over the middle finger (**Fig 9**).

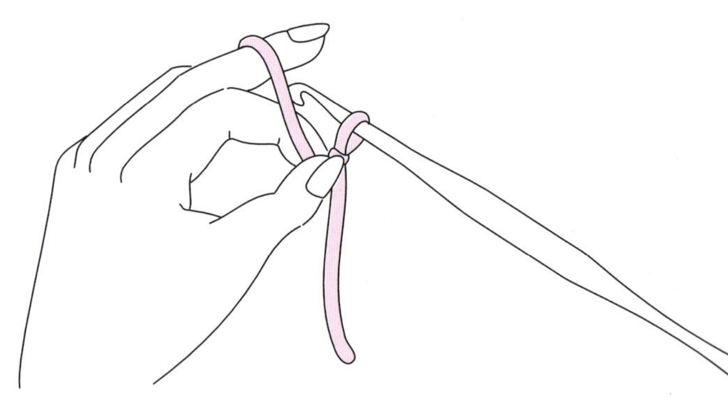

Fig 9

and under the remaining fingers of the left hand (**Fig 9a**).

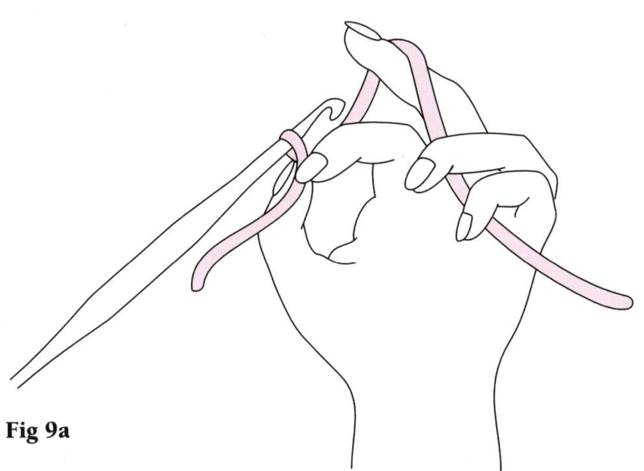

Fig 9a

Your middle finger will stick up a bit to help the thread feed smoothly from the ball; the other fingers help maintain even tension on the thread as you work.

Hint: As you practice, you can adjust the way your left hand holds the thread to whatever is most comfortable for you.

Step 2: Bring the thread over the hook from back to front and hook it (**Fig 10**).

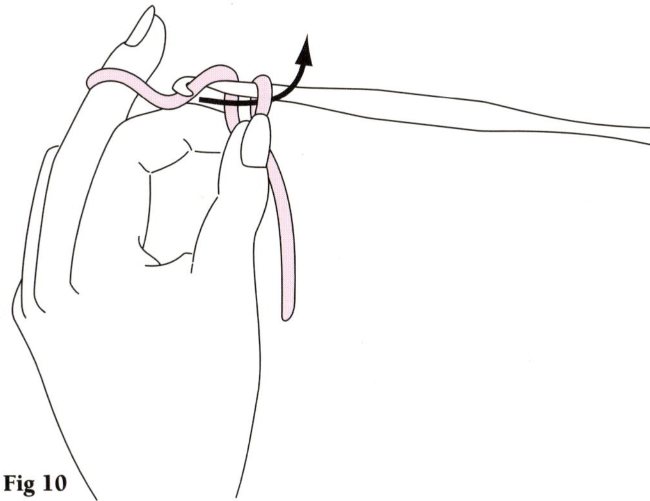

Fig 10

Draw hooked thread through the loop of the slip knot on the hook and up onto the working area of the hook (see arrow on **Fig 10**); you have now made one chain stitch (**Fig 11**).

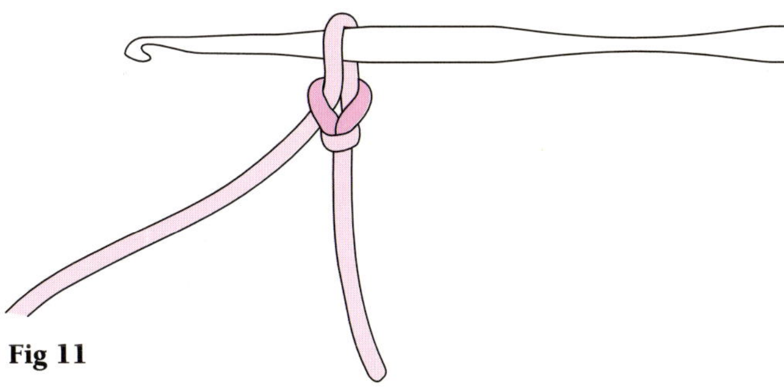

Fig 11

Step 3: Again bring the thread over the hook from back to front (**Fig 12**).

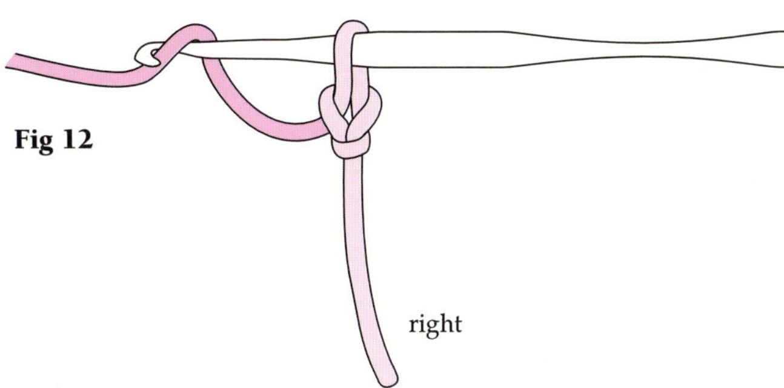

Fig 12

Note: Take care not to bring thread from front to back (**Fig 12a**).

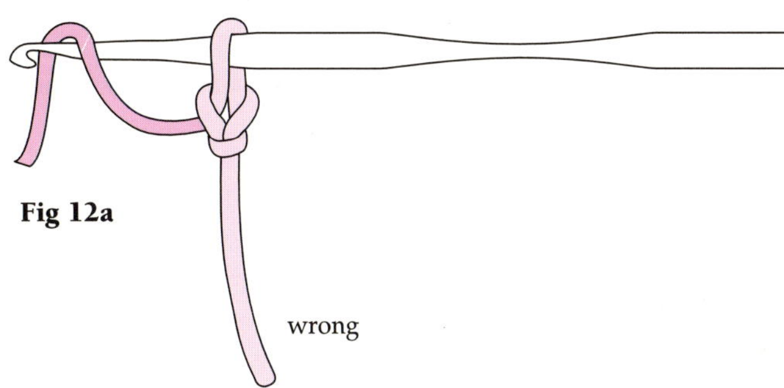

Fig 12a

Hook it and draw through loop on the hook: you have made another chain stitch (**Fig 13**).

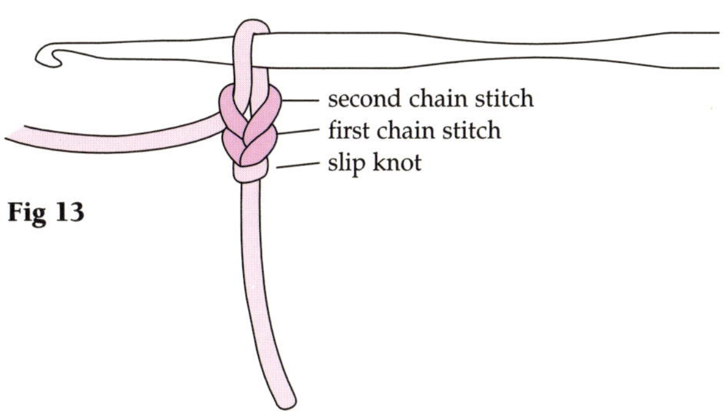

Fig 13

Repeat Step 3 for each additional chain stitch, being careful to move the left thumb and index finger up the chain close to the hook after each new stitch or two (**Fig 14**). This helps you control the work. Also be sure to pull each new stitch up onto the working area of the hook.

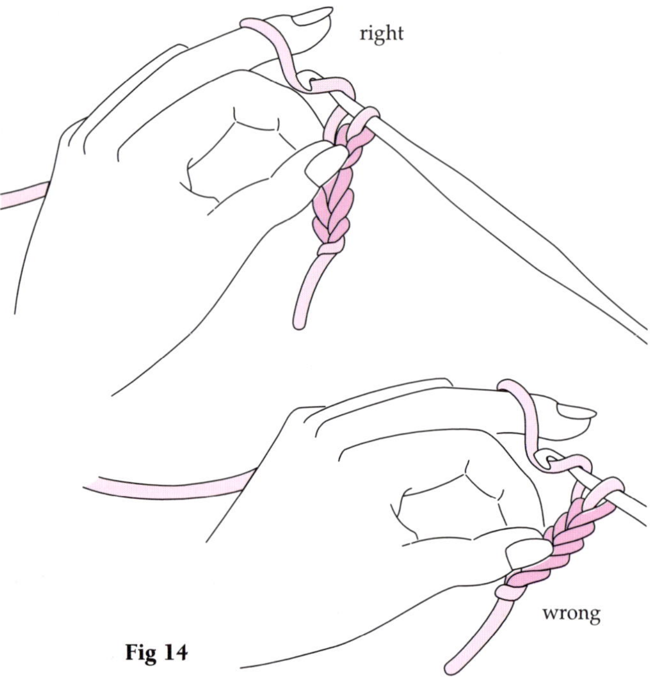

Fig 14

The working thread and the work in progress are always held in your left hand.

Practice making chains until you are comfortable with your grip of the hook and the flow of the thread; in the beginning your work will be uneven, with some chain stitches loose and others tight. While you're learning, try to keep the chain stitches loose. As your skill increases, the chain should be firm, but not tight, with all chain stitches even in size.

Hint: As you practice, if the hook slips out of a stitch, don't get upset! Just insert the hook again from the front into the center of the last stitch, taking care not to twist the loop (**Fig 15**).

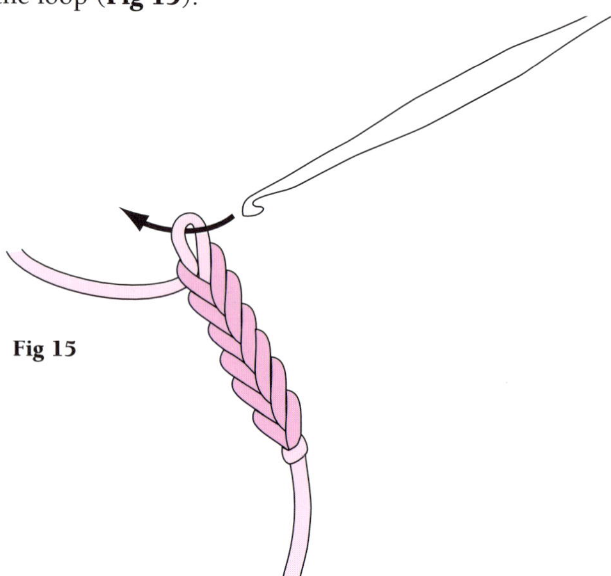

Fig 15

When you are comfortable with the chain stitch, draw your hook out of the last stitch, and pull out the work back to the beginning. Now you've learned the important first step of crochet: the beginning chain.

Lesson 3: Working into the Chain

Once you have worked the beginning chain, you are ready to begin the stitches required to make any project. These stitches are worked into the starting chain. For practice, make 6 chains loosely.

Hint: When counting your chain stitches at the start of a pattern – which you must do very carefully before continuing – note that the loop on the hook is never counted as a stitch; and the starting slip knot is never counted as a stitch (**Fig 16**).

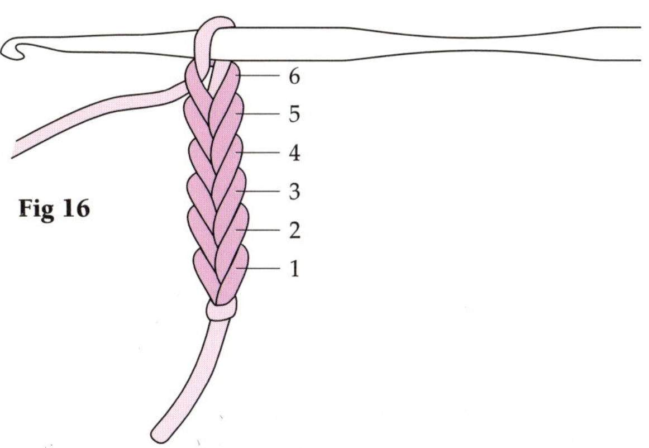

Fig 16

Now stop and look at the chain. The front looks like a series of interlocking V's (**Fig 16**), and each stitch has a bump or ridge at the back (**Fig 17**).

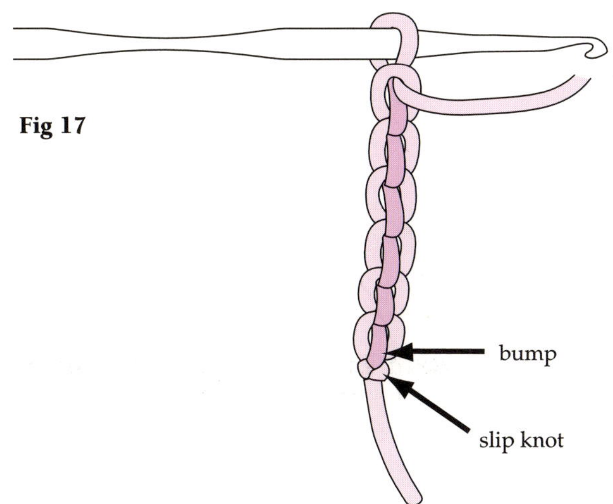

Fig 17

You will never work into the first chain from the hook. Depending on the stitch, you will work into the second, third, fourth, etc. chain from the hook. The instructions will always state how many chains to skip before starting the first stitch.

When working a stitch, insert hook from the front of the chain, through the center of a V stitch, and under the corresponding bump on the back of the same stitch (**Fig 18**).

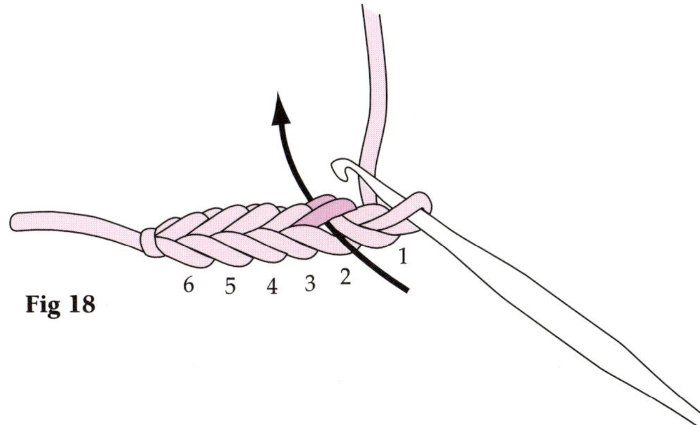

Fig 18

Excluding the first stitch, you will work into every stitch in the chain unless the pattern states differently, but not into the beginning slip knot (**Fig 18a**). Be sure that you do not skip that last chain at the end.

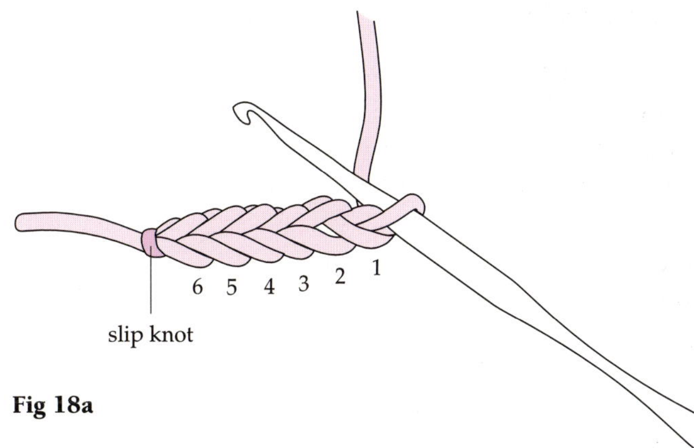

Fig 18a

Lesson 4: Single Crochet (abbreviated sc)

Most crochet is made with variations of just four different stitches: single crochet, double crochet, half double crochet, and triple crochet. The stitches differ mainly in height, which is varied by the number of times the thread is wrapped around the hook. The shortest and most basic of these stitches is the single crochet.

Working Row 1

To practice, begin with the chain of 6 stitches made in Lesson 3 and work the first row of single crochet as follows:

Step 1: Skip first chain stitch from hook. Insert hook in the 2nd chain stitch through the center of the V and under the back bump; with third finger of your left hand, bring thread over the hook from back to front, and hook the thread (**Fig 19**).

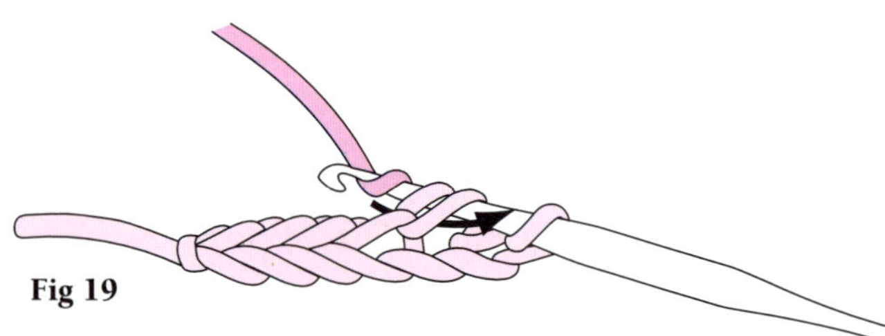

Fig 19

Draw thread through the chain stitch and well up onto the working area of the hook. You now have 2 loops on the hook (**Fig 20**).

Fig 20

Step 2: Again bring thread over the hook from back to front, hook it and draw it through both loops on the hook (**Fig 21**).

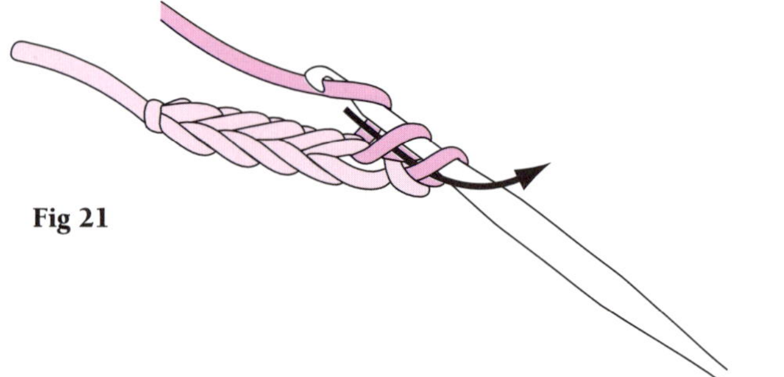

Fig 21

One loop will remain on the hook, and you have made one single crochet (**Fig 22**).

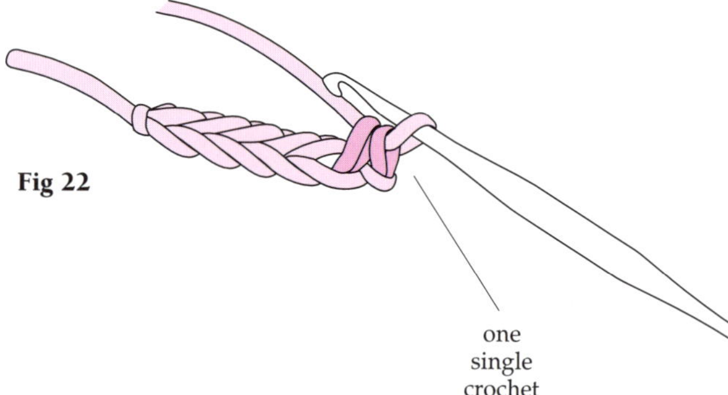

Fig 22

Step 3: Insert hook in next chain stitch as before, hook thread, and draw it through the chain stitch; hook thread again and draw it through both loops: you have made another single crochet.

Repeat Step 3 in each remaining chain stitch, taking care to work in the last chain stitch, **but not in the slip knot**. You have completed one row of single crochet, and should have 5 stitches in the row. **Fig 23** shows how to count the stitches.

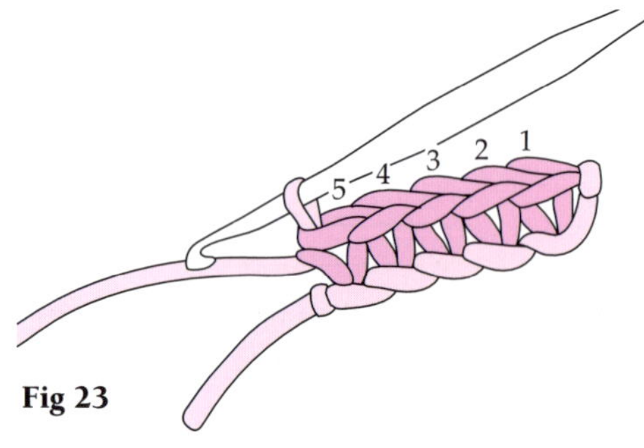

Fig 23

Hint: As you work, be careful not to twist the chain; keep all the V's facing you.

Working Row 2

To work the second row of single crochet, you need to bring the thread up to the correct height to work the first stitch, and then turn the work so you can work back across the first row. To raise the thread, chain 1 (this is called a turning chain), and then turn the work in the direction of the arrow (counterclockwise) as shown in **Fig 24**.

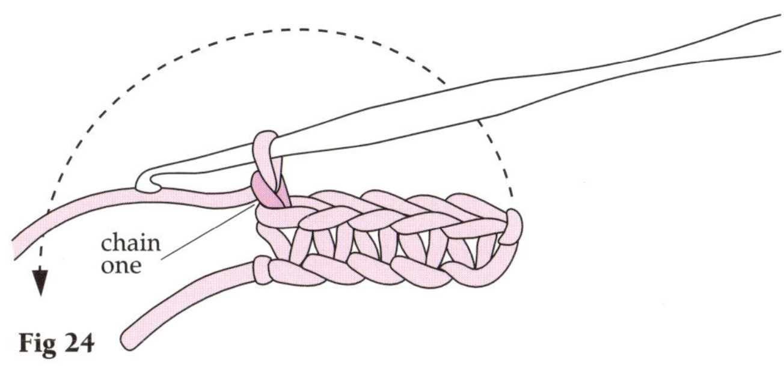

Fig 24

Do not remove the hook from the loop as you do this (**Fig 24a**).

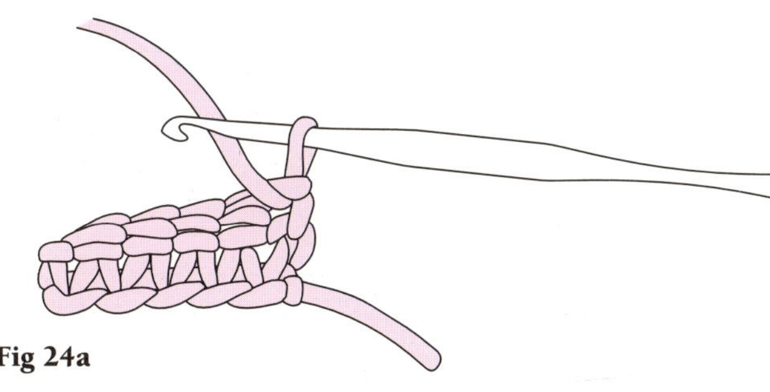
Fig 24a

This row, and all the following rows of single crochet, will be worked into a previous row of single crochet, not into the beginning chain as you did before. Remember that when you worked into the starting chain, you inserted the hook through the center of the V, and under the bump. This is only done when working into a starting chain.

To work into a previous row of crochet, insert the hook under both loops of the previous stitch, as shown in **Fig 25**, instead of through the center of the V.

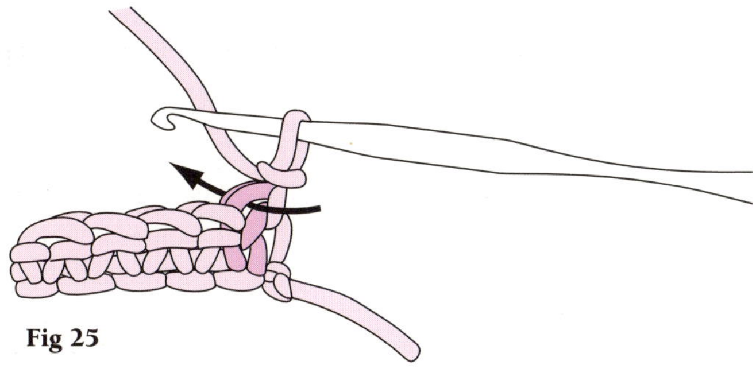
Fig 25

The first single crochet of the row is worked in the last stitch of the previous row (**Fig 25**), not into the turning chain. Work a single crochet in each single crochet to the end, taking care to work in each stitch, especially the last stitch, which is easy to miss (**Fig 26**).

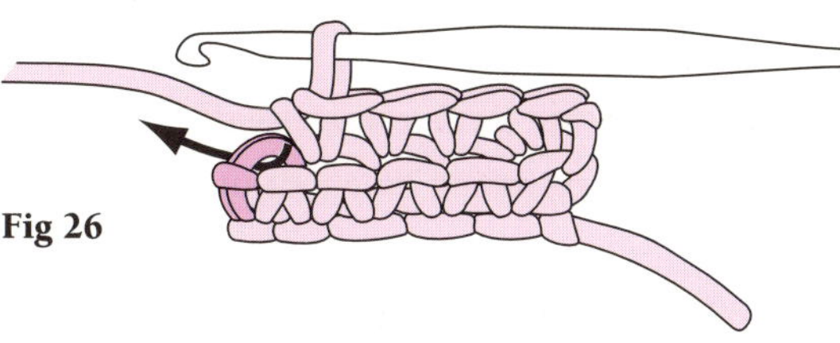
Fig 26

Stop now and count your stitches; you should still have 5 single crochets on the row (**Fig 27**).

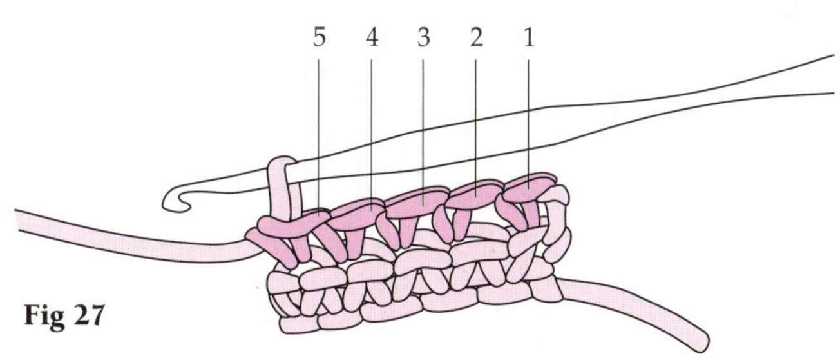

Fig 27

Hint: When you want to pause to count stitches, check your work, have a snack or chat on the phone, you can remove your hook from the work — but do this at the end of a row, not in the middle. To remove the hook, pull straight up on the hook to make a long loop (**Fig 28**).

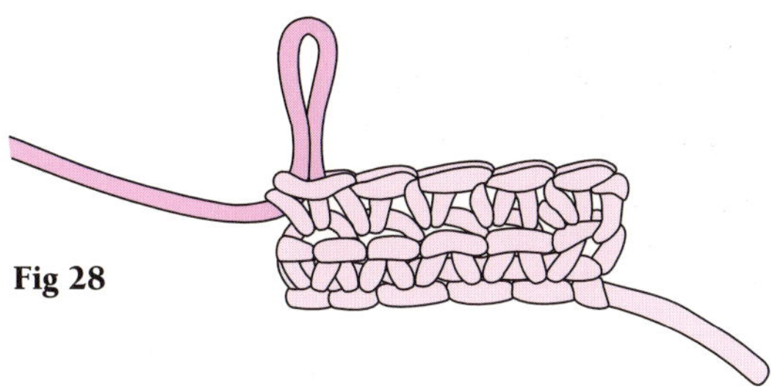
Fig 28

Then withdraw the hook and put it on a table or other safe place (sofas and chairs have a habit of eating crochet hooks). Put work in a safe place so loop is not pulled out. To begin work again, just insert the hook in the big loop (don't twist the loop), and pull on the thread from the ball to tighten the loop.

To end Row 2, after the last single crochet, chain 1 for the turning chain, and turn the work counterclockwise.

Here is the way instructions for Row 2 might be written in a pattern:

Row 2: Sc in each sc; ch 1, turn.

Note: To save space, a number of abbreviations are used.

For a list of abbreviations used in patterns, see page 22.

Working Row 3

Row 3 is worked exactly as you worked Row 2. Here are the instructions as they would be given in a pattern:

Row 3: Rep Row 2.

Now wasn't that easy? For practice, work three more rows, which means you will repeat Row 2 three times more.

Hint: Try to keep your stitches as smooth and even as possible; remember to work loosely rather than tightly, and to make each stitch well up on the working area of the hook. Be sure to chain 1 and turn at the end of each row, and to check carefully to be sure you've worked into the last stitch of each row.

Count the stitches at the end of each row; do you still have 5? Good work.

Hint: What if you don't have 5 stitches at the end of a row? Perhaps you worked two stitches in one stitch, or skipped a stitch. Find your mistake, then just pull out your stitches back to the mistake; pulling out in crochet is simple. Just take out the hook, and gently pull on the thread. The stitches will come out easily; when you reach the place where you want to start again, insert the hook in the last loop (taking care not to twist it) and begin.

Finishing Off

It's time to move on to another stitch, so let's finish off your single crochet practice piece, which you can keep for future reference. After the last stitch of the last row, cut the thread, leaving a 4" end. As you did when you took your hook out for a break, draw the hook straight up, but this time draw the thread cut end completely through the stitch. **Photo A** shows an actual sample of six rows of single crochet to which you can compare your practice rows and shows how to count the stitches and rows.

Now you can put the piece away, and it won't pull out (you might want to tag this piece as a sample of single crochet).

Photo A

Lesson 5: Double Crochet (abbreviated dc)

Double crochet is a taller stitch than single crochet. To practice, first chain 14 stitches loosely. Then work the first row of double crochet as follows:

Working Row 1

Step 1: Bring thread once over the hook from back to front (as though you were going to make another chain stitch); skip the first three chains from the hook, then insert hook in the 4th chain (**Fig 29**).

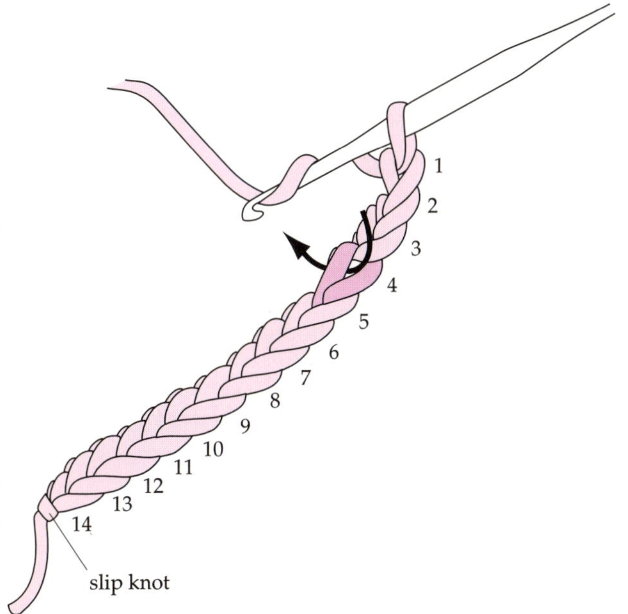

Fig 29

Remember not to count the loop on the hook as a chain. Be sure to go through the center of the V of the chain, and under the bump at the back, and to not twist the chain.

Step 2: Hook thread and draw it through the chain stitch and up onto the working area of the hook: you now have 3 loops on the hook (**Fig 30**).

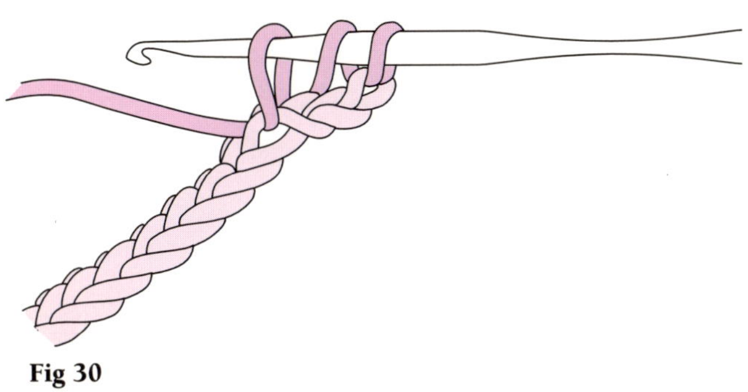

Fig 30

Step 3: Hook thread and draw through the first 2 loops on the hook (**Fig 31**).

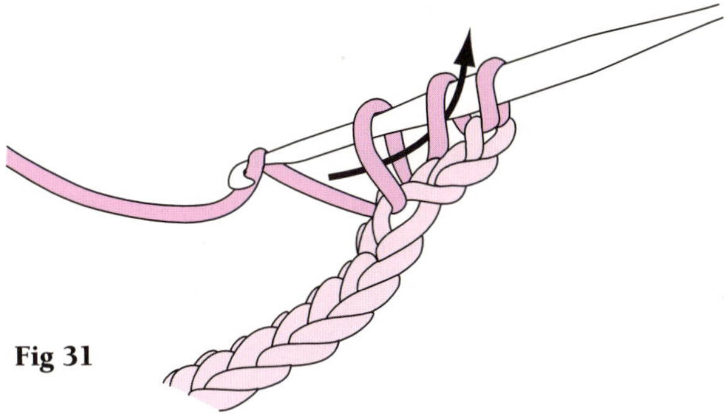

Fig 31

You now have 2 loops on the hook (**Fig 32**).

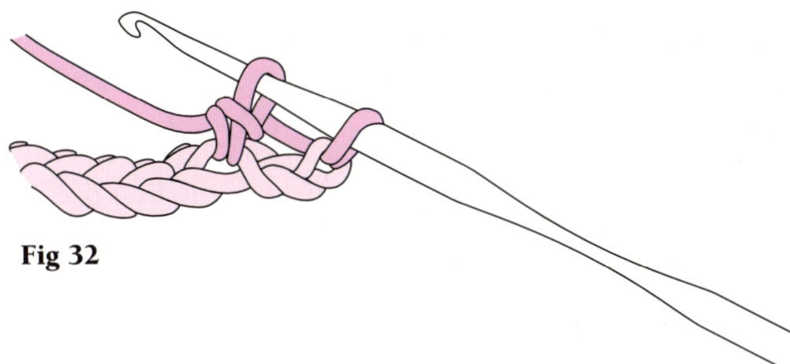

Fig 32

Step 4: Hook thread and draw through both loops on the hook (**Fig 33**).

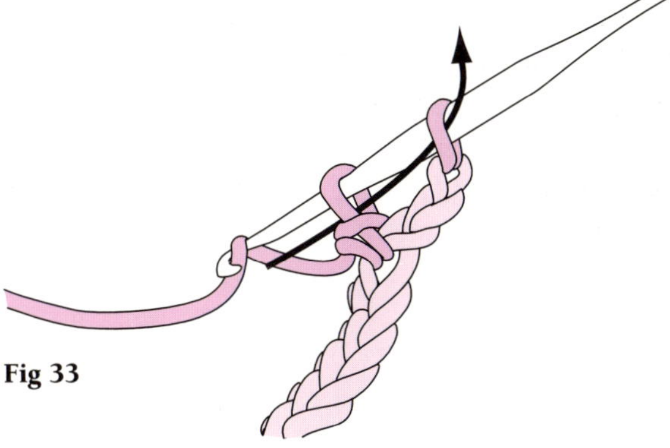

Fig 33

You have now completed one double crochet and one loop remains on the hook (**Fig 34**).

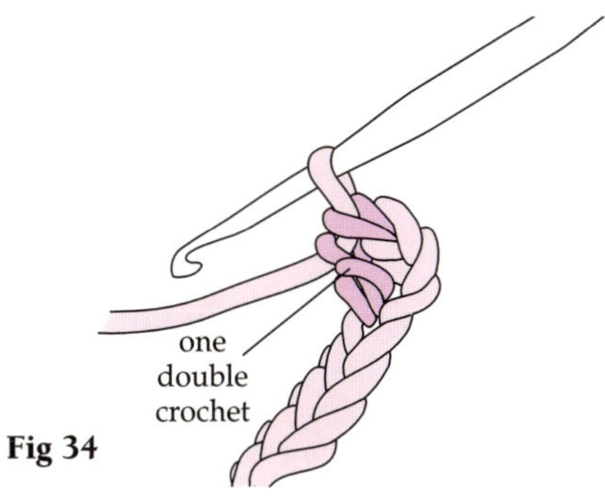

Fig 34

Repeat Steps 1 through 4 in each chain stitch across (except in Step 1, work in next chain, don't skip 3 chains).

When you've worked a double crochet in the last chain, pull out your hook and look at your work, then count your double crochet stitches: there should be 12 of them, counting the first 3 chain stitches you skipped at the beginning of the row as a double crochet (**Fig 35**).

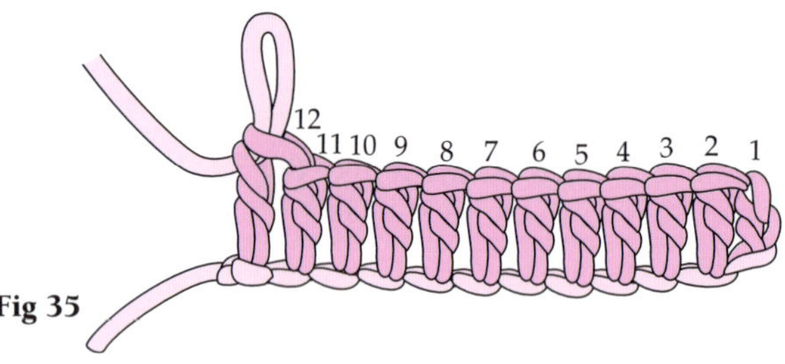

Fig 35

Hint: In working double crochet on a beginning chain row, the 3 chains skipped before making the first double crochet are always counted as a double crochet stitch.

You need to bring the thread up to the correct height for the next row, and then turn the work. So to raise the thread, chain 3 (this is called the turning chain); then turn the work counterclockwise before beginning Row 2.

Working Row 2

The 3 chains in the turning chain just made count as the first double crochet of the new row, so skip the first double crochet and work a double crochet in the second stitch (being sure to insert hook under top 2 loops of stitch): **Fig 36** indicates the right and wrong placement of this stitch.

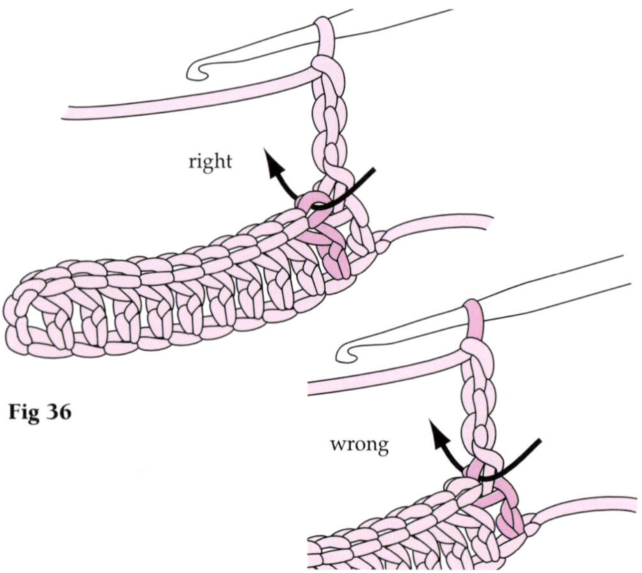

Fig 36

Work a double crochet in each remaining stitch across previous row, and be sure at the end of the row to work the last double crochet in the top of the turning chain from the previous row. Be sure to insert hook in the center of the V (and back bump) of the top chain of the turning chain (**Fig 37**). Stop and count your double crochets; there should be 12 stitches. Now, chain 3 and turn.

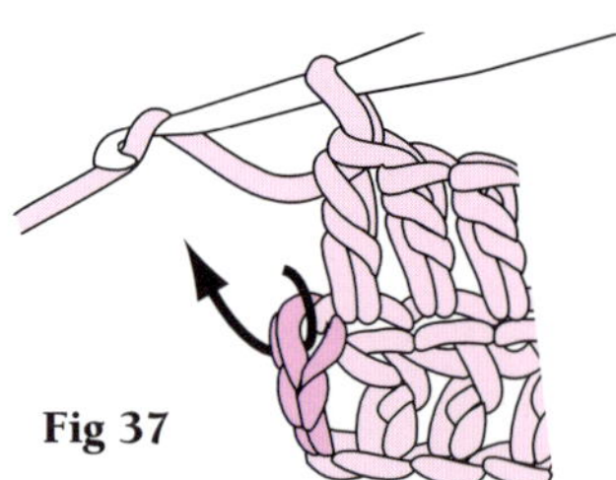
Fig 37

Here is the way the instructions might be written in a pattern:

Row 2: Dc in each dc: you should have 12 dc; ch 3, turn.

Working Row 3

Row 3 is worked exactly as you worked Row 2.

In a pattern, instructions would read:

Row 3: Rep Row 2.

For practice, work 3 more rows, repeating Row 2. At the end of the last row, finish off the piece as you did for the single crochet practice piece. **Photo B** shows a sample of 6 rows of double crochet and how to count the stitches and rows.

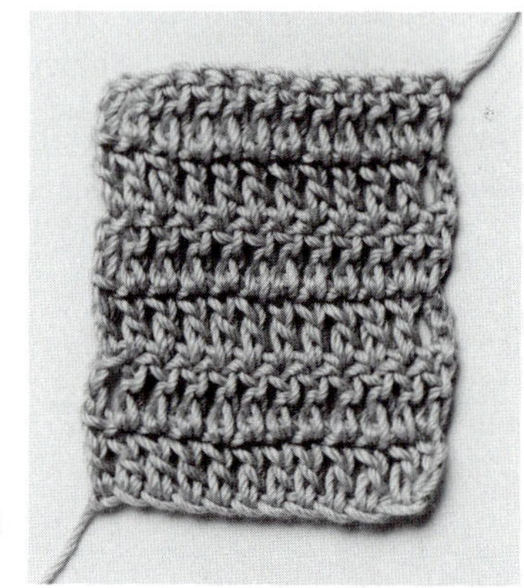
Photo B

Break Time!

Now you have learned the two most often used stitches in crochet. Since you've worked so hard, it's time to take a break. Walk around, relax your hands, have a snack, or just take a few minutes to release the stress that sometimes develops when learning something new.

Lesson 6: Half Double Crochet (abbreviated hdc)

Just as its name implies, this stitch eliminates one step of double crochet, and works up about half as tall.

To practice, chain 13 stitches loosely.

Working Row 1

Step l: Bring thread once over hook from back to front, skip the first 2 chains, then insert hook in the third chain from the hook (**Fig 38**).

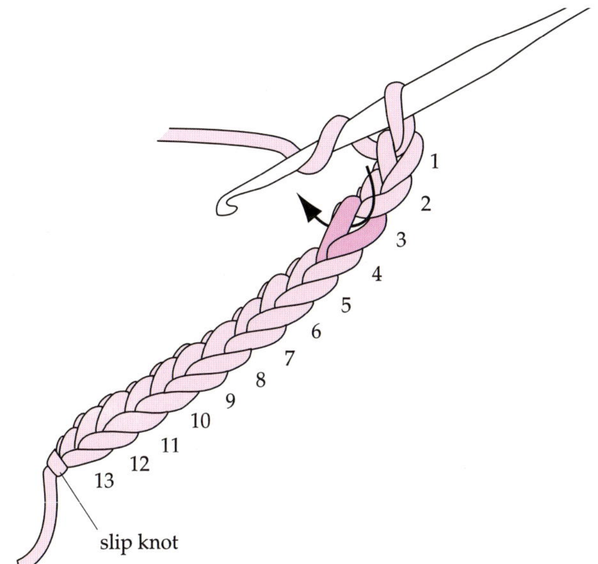

Fig 38

Remember not to count the loop on the hook as a chain.

Step 2: Hook thread and draw it through the chain stitch and up onto the working area of the hook. You now have 3 loops on the hook (**Fig 39**).

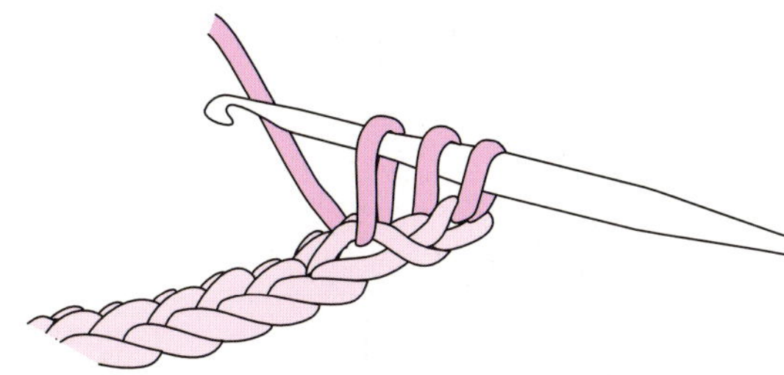

Fig 39

Step 3: Hook thread and draw it through all 3 loops on the hook in one motion (**Fig 40**).

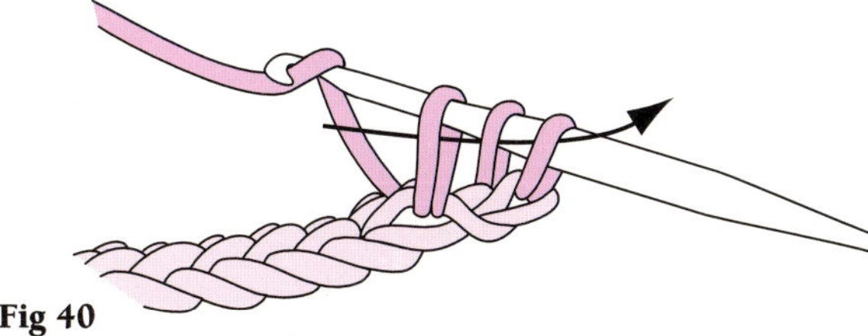

Fig 40

You have completed one half double crochet and one loop remains on the hook (**Fig 41**).

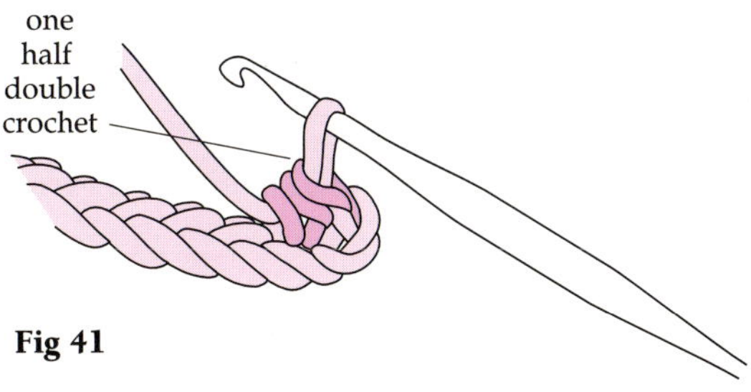

Fig 41

In next chain stitch work a half double crochet as follows:

Step l: Bring thread once over hook from back to front, insert hook in next chain.

Repeat Steps 2 and 3 of Row 1.

Repeat the previous 3 steps in each remaining chain stitch across. Stop and count your stitches; you should have 12 half double crochets, counting the first 2 chains you skipped at the beginning of the row as a half double crochet (**Fig 42**).

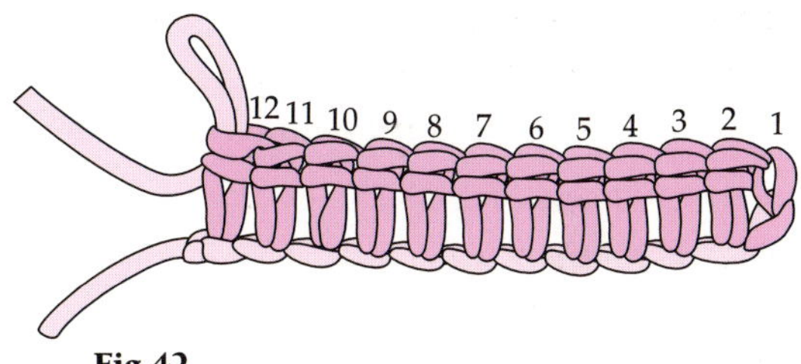

Fig 42

Chain 2 and turn.

Working Row 2

Like double crochet, the turning chain does count as a stitch in half double crochet (unless your pattern specifies otherwise). Skip the first half double crochet of the previous row and work a half double crochet in the second stitch (**Fig 43**) and in each remaining stitch across the previous row. At the end of the row, chain 2 and turn.

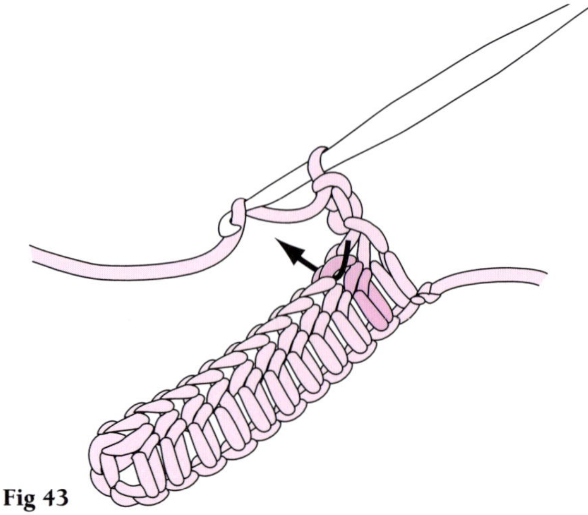

Fig 43

Here is the way the instructions might be written in a pattern:

Row 2: Hdc in each hdc: you should have 12 hdc; ch 2, turn.

Working Row 3

Row 3 is worked exactly as you worked Row 2.

In a pattern, instructions would read:

Row 3: Rep Row 2.

For practice, work 3 more rows, repeating Row 2. Be sure to count your stitches carefully at the end of each row. When the practice rows are completed, finish off. **Photo C** shows a sample of 6 rows of half double crochet and how to count the stitches and the rows. Continue with the next lesson.

Photo C

Lesson 7: Triple Crochet (abbreviated trc)

Triple crochet is a tall stitch that works up quickly and is fun to do. Sometimes in instructions it is called treble crochet. To practice, first chain 15 stitches loosely. Then work the first row as follows:

Working Row 1

Step 1: Bring thread over the hook twice (from back to front), skip the first four chains, then insert hook into the 5th chain from the hook (**Fig 44**).

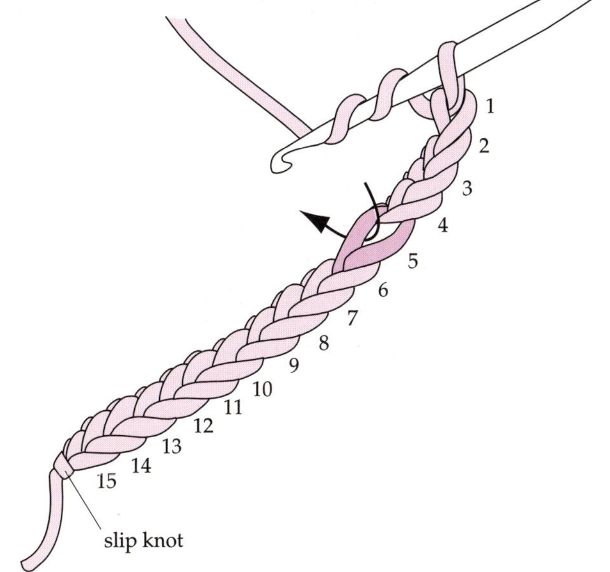

Fig 44

Step 2: Hook thread and draw it through the chain stitch and up onto the working area of the hook; you now have 4 loops on the hook (**Fig 45**).

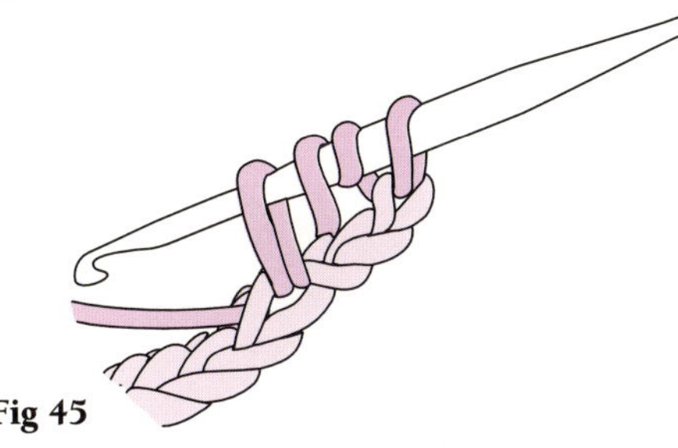

Fig 45

Step 3: Hook thread and draw it through the first 2 loops on the hook (**Fig 46**).

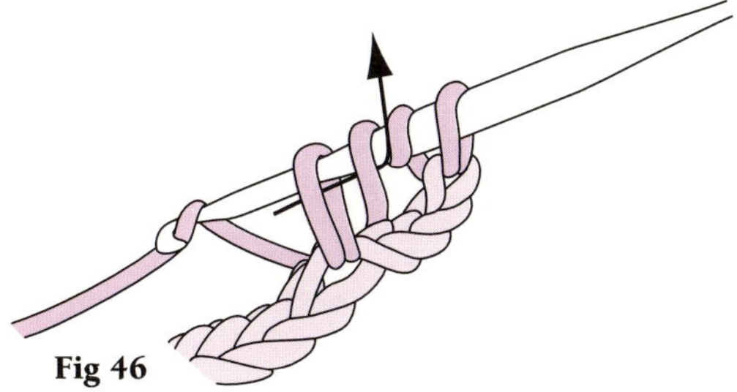

Fig 46

You now have 3 loops on the hook (**Fig 46a**).

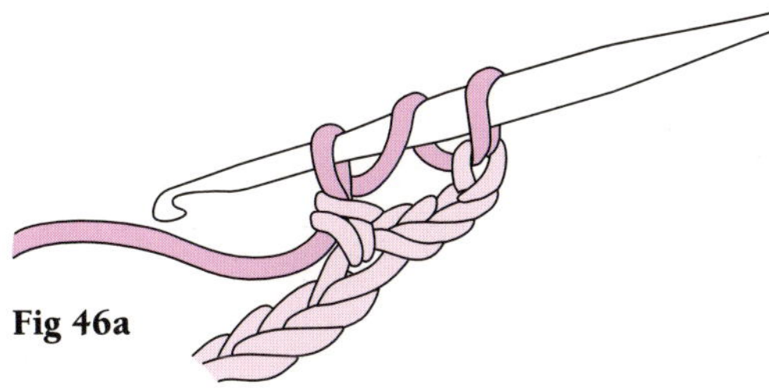

Fig 46a

Step 4: Hook thread again and draw it through the next 2 loops on the hook (**Fig 47**).

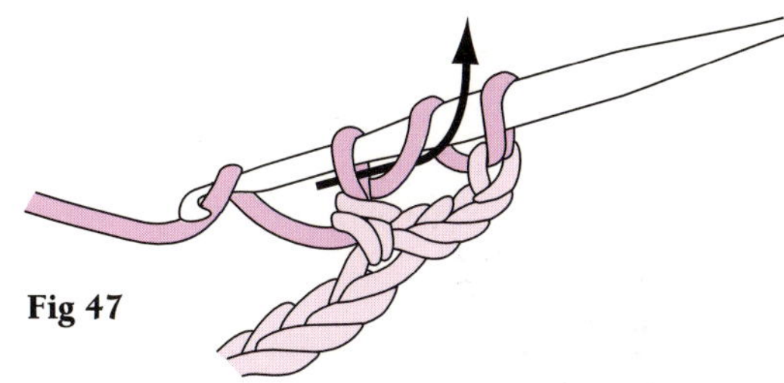

Fig 47

2 loops remain on the hook (**Fig 47a**).

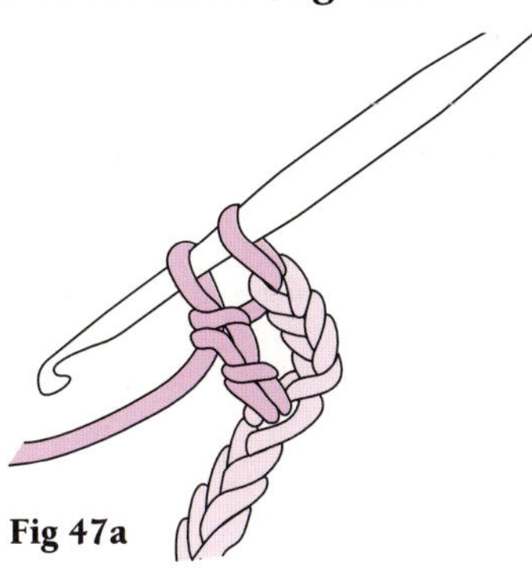

Fig 47a

Step 5: Hook thread and draw it through both remaining loops on the hook (**Fig 48**).

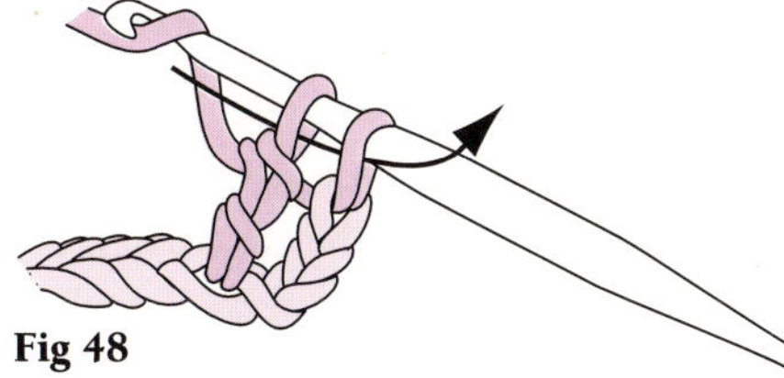

Fig 48

You have now completed one triple crochet and one loop remains on the hook (**Fig 49**).

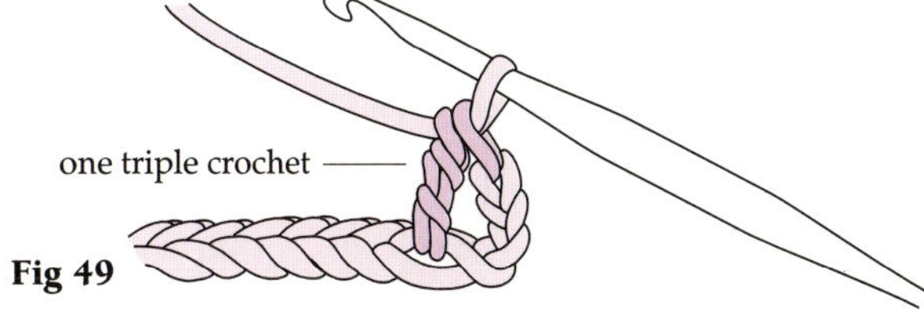

Fig 49

In next chain stitch work a triple crochet as follows:

Step 1: Bring thread over the hook twice (from back to front), insert hook in the next chain (**Fig 50**).

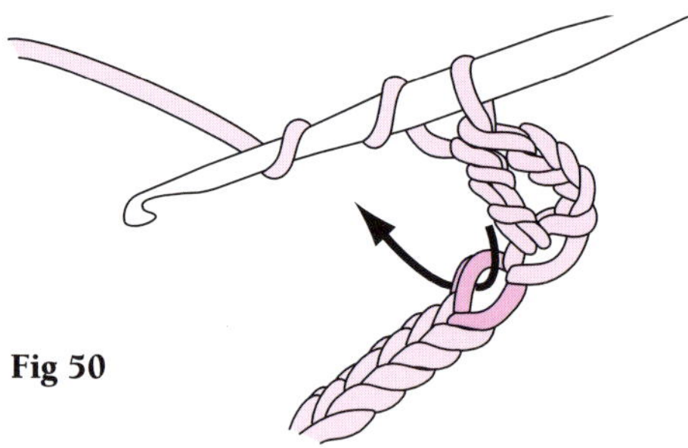

Fig 50

Steps 2 through 5: Repeat the preceding Steps 2 through 5.

Repeat the previous 5 steps in each remaining chain stitch across.

When you've worked a triple crochet in the last chain, count your stitches: there should be 12 of them, counting the first 4 chains you skipped at the beginning of the row as a triple crochet (**Fig 51**); chain 4 and turn.

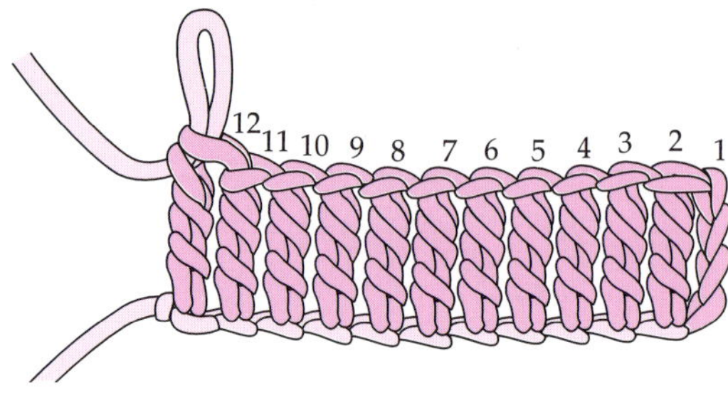

Fig 51

Hint: In working the first row of triple crochet, the 4 chains skipped before making the first triple crochet are always counted as a triple crochet stitch.

Working Row 2

The 4 turning chains have brought your thread up to the correct height, and count as the first stitch of the row. So skip the first stitch, and work a triple crochet in the second stitch (**Fig 52**).

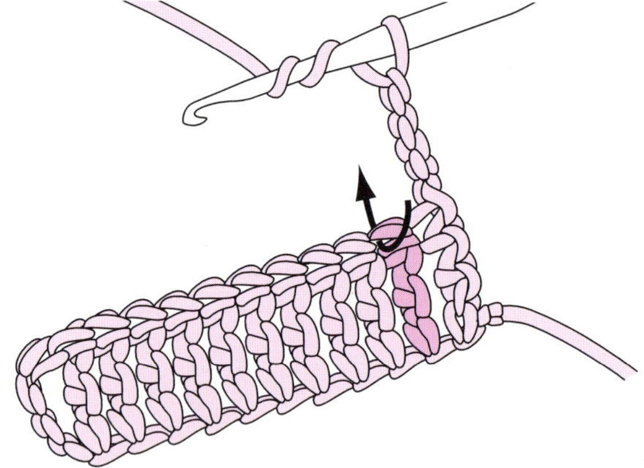

Fig 52

Work a triple crochet in each remaining stitch across previous row, being sure at end to work last triple crochet in the top of the turning chain from the previous row. Count stitches; be sure you still have 12 stitches; chain 4 and turn.

Hint: Remember to work last trc of each row in turning chain of previous row. Missing this stitch in the turning chain is a common error.

Here is the way the instructions might be written in a pattern:

Row 2: Trc in each trc: you should have 12 trc; ch 4, turn.

Working Row 3

Work Row 3 exactly as you worked Row 2.

For practice, work 3 more rows, repeating Row 2. At the end of the last row, finish off the piece. **Photo D** shows a sample of 6 rows of triple crochet and how to count the stitches and rows.

Photo D

Lesson 8: Slip Stitch (abbreviated sl st)

This is the shortest of all crochet stitches, and is really more a technique than a stitch. Slip stitches are usually used to move thread across a group of stitches without adding height, or to join work.

Moving Thread Across Stitches

Chain 10.

Working Row 1

Double crochet in the 4th chain from hook (see page 9) and in each chain across. On the next row, you are going to slip stitch across the first four stitches before beginning to work double crochet again. So instead of making 3 chains for the turning chain as you would usually do for a second row of double crochet, this time just chain 1 and turn.

Working Row 2

The turning ch-1 does not count as a stitch; therefore insert hook under both loops of first stitch, hook thread, and draw it through both loops of stitch and loop on the hook (**Fig 53**): one slip stitch made.

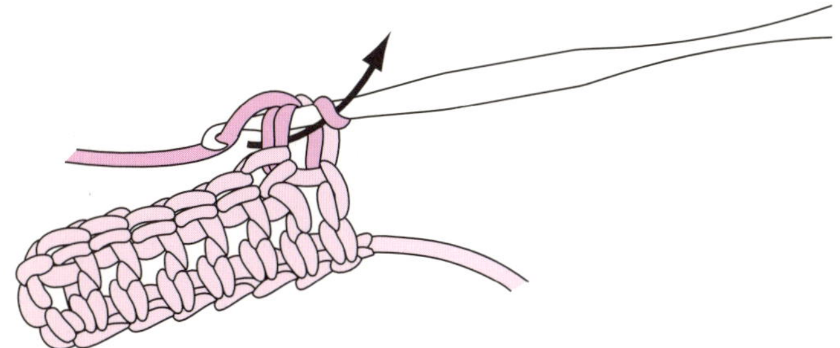

Fig 53

Work a slip stitch in the same manner in each of the next 3 stitches. Now we're going to finish the row in double crochet; chain 3 to get thread at the right height (the chain 3 counts as a double crochet), then work a double crochet in each of the remaining stitches. Look at your work and see how we moved the thread across with slip stitches, adding very little height (**Fig 54**).

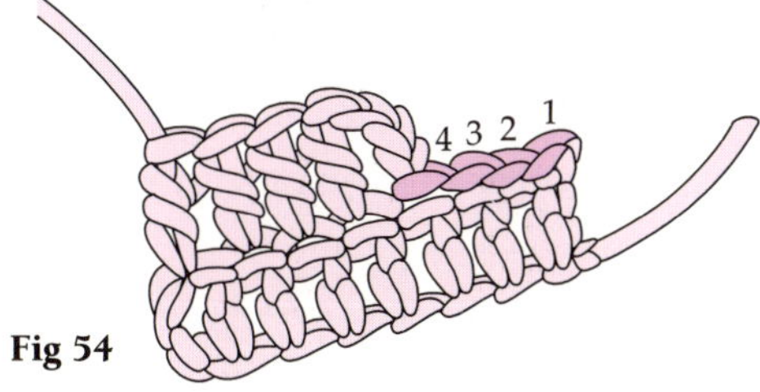

Fig 54

Finish off and save the sample.

Here is the way the instructions might be written in a pattern.

Row 2: Sl st in next 4 dc; ch 3, dc in each rem dc: 5 dc. Finish off.

Hint: When slip stitching across stitches, always work very loosely.

Joining Stitches

Joining a chain into a circle.

Chain 6, then insert hook through the first chain you made (next to the slip knot, **Fig 55**).

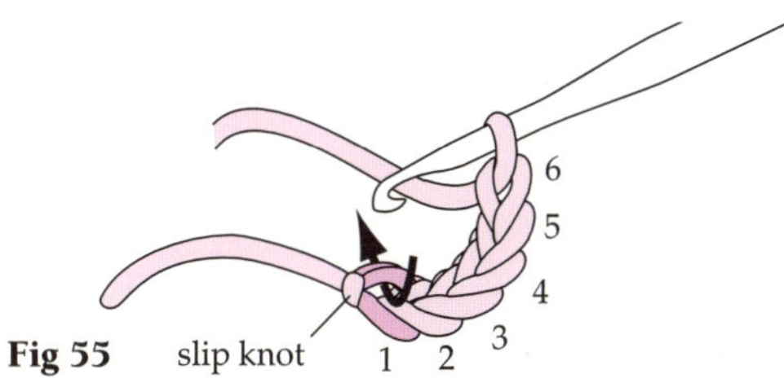

Fig 55

Hook thread and draw it through the chain and through the loop on hook; you have now joined the 6 chains into a circle or ring. This is the way many motifs and doilies are started. Cut thread and keep this practice piece as a sample.

Joining the end of a round to the beginning of the same round.

Chain 6; join with a slip stitch in first chain you made to form a ring. Chain 3, work 11 double crochet in ring; insert hook in 3rd chain of beginning chain 3 (**Fig 56**), hook thread and draw it through the chain and through the loop on the hook; you have now joined the round. Cut thread and keep this piece as a sample.

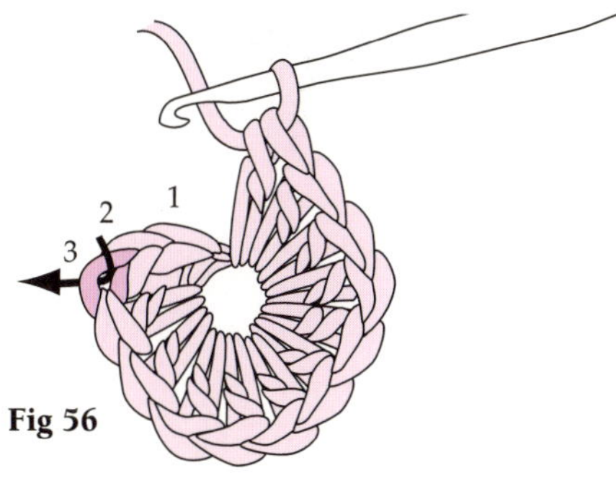

Fig 56

Here is the way the instructions might be written in a pattern:

Rnd 1: Ch 3, 11 dc in ring; join in 3rd ch of beg ch-3.

Lesson 9: Stitch Sampler

You've now learned the basic stitches of crochet – and wasn't it fun? The hard part is over!

To help you understand the difference in the way single crochet, half double crochet, double crochet and triple crochet stitches are worked, and the difference in their heights, let's make one more sample.

Chain 17 stitches loosely. Taking care not to work too tightly, single crochet in the second chain from hook and in each of the next three chains; work a half double crochet in each of the next four chains; work a double crochet in each of the next four chains; work a triple crochet in each of the next four chains; finish off. Your work should look like **Photo E**.

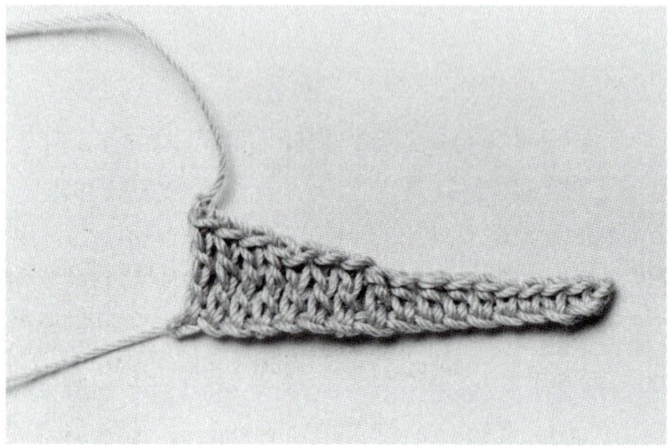

Photo E

Lesson 10: Pattern Stitches

Pattern stitches are groups of two or more crochet stitches, or sometimes a series of rows or rounds, which form a pattern. Instructions for pattern stitches are usually given before the project instructions begin. Here are three examples.

Cluster (CL):

A cluster is made by joining two or more stitches to make one stitch. Here is the way the instructions might be written in a pattern:

(YO, draw up lp in next st, YO, draw through 2 lps on hook) 3 times (**Fig 57**); YO and draw through all 4 lps on hook (**Fig 58**): CL made.

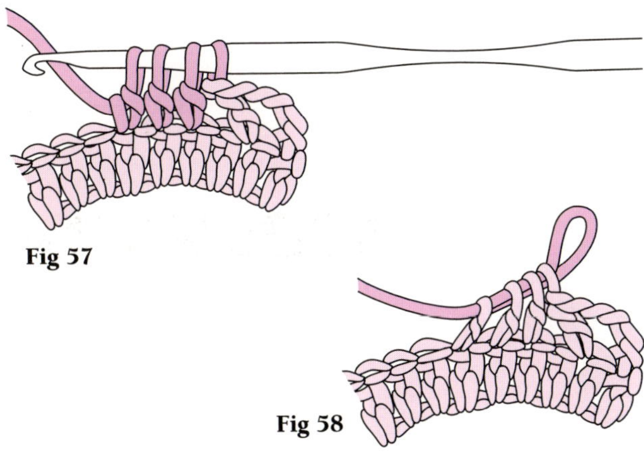

Fig 57

Fig 58

The cluster has joined three stitches into one stitch.

Fig 59 shows two CLs and a ch-3 lp. The ch-3 lp replaces the two decreased stitches and the skipped stitch between the CLs. Here is how this section might be written in a pattern:

. . .; CL over next 3 dc; ch 3, CL over next 3 dc; . . .

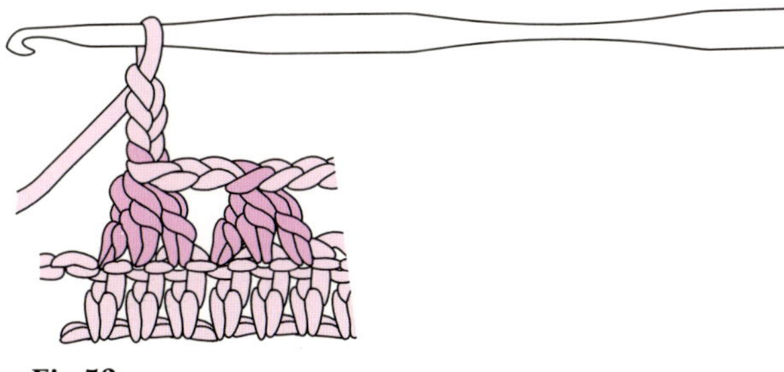

Fig 59

Popcorn (PC):

Popcorn stitches are made by drawing several stitches together after they have been made, causing a bunching or popcorn affect on one side of the work. Here is the way the instructions might be written in a pattern:

4 dc in next st; remove hook from lp, insert hook in first dc made, hook dropped lp and draw through (**Fig 60**): PC made.

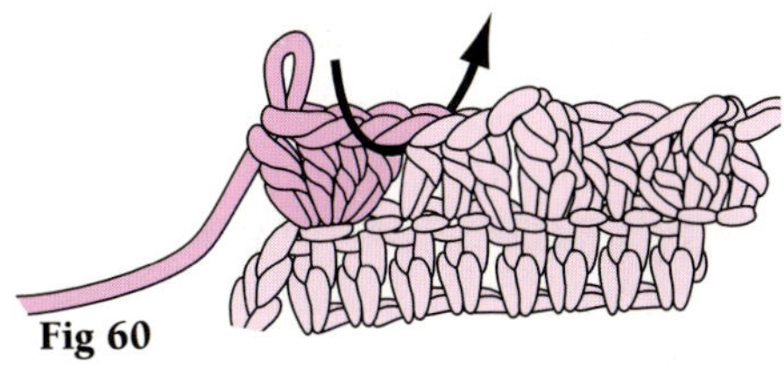

Fig 60

Picot:

Picots are little loops most often worked in the last round of a project to add a finished look. They can also be added within the pattern. Picots are made by chaining a specified number of chains, then working a sl st into the first chain, or into the top of the last stitch worked. Here is the way the instructions might be written in a pattern:

Ch 3, sl st in first ch: picot made; . . . **Fig 61** shows a completed picot, and a second picot about to be completed.

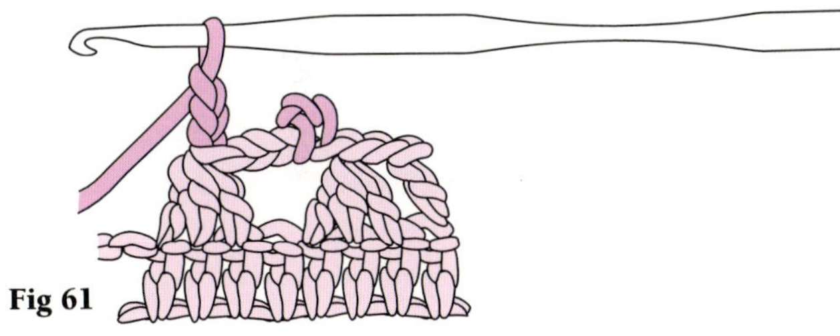

Fig 61

Pineapple:

Since the pineapple is a symbol of hospitality, it is the favored pattern stitch of most thread crocheters. Several pineapples spreading outward on a doily or bordering a tablecloth are in themselves a work of art.

Because several rows or rounds must be worked to complete a pineapple, the instructions are written into the pattern. Pineapples usually begin with a group of stitches worked together to form a base. **Photo F** is an example of a pineapple design.

Photo F

Now in 10 easy lessons you've become a crocheter! You're ready to start your first project – will it be a doily, a pretty trim for your linens, a snowflake for your window or Christmas tree, or a tablecloth or a bedspread? Be sure to read the following section on Special Helps before you start.

Special Helps

Increasing and Decreasing

Shaping is done by increasing, which adds stitches to make the crocheted piece wider; or decreasing, which subtracts stitches to make the piece narrower.

Note: Make a practice sample by chaining 15 loosely and working 4 rows of single crochet with 14 stitches in each row. Do not finish off at end of last row. Use this sample swatch to practice the following method of increasing stitches.

Increasing: To increase one stitch in single, half double, double or triple crochet, simply work two stitches in one stitch. For example, if you are working in single crochet and you need to increase one stitch, you would work one single crochet in the next stitch; then you would work another single crochet in the same stitch.

For practice: On sample swatch, chain 1 and turn. Single crochet in first 2 stitches; increase in next stitch by working 2 single crochets in stitch (**Fig 62**).

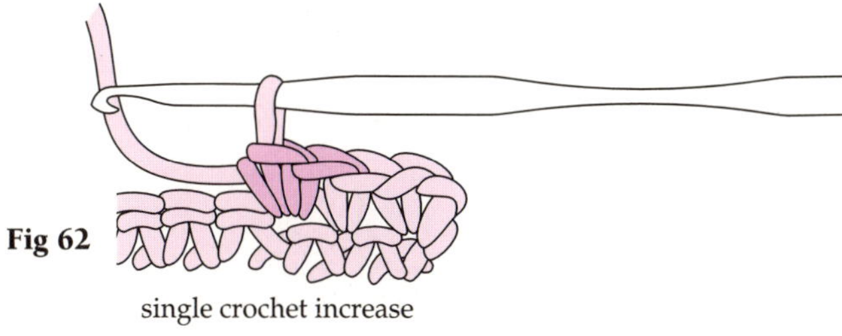

Fig 62

single crochet increase

Repeat increase in each stitch across row to last 2 stitches; single crochet in each of next 2 stitches. Count your stitches; you should have 24 stitches. If you don't have 24 stitches, examine your swatch to see if you have increased in each specified stitch. Rework the row if necessary.

Increases in half double, double and triple crochet are shown in **Fig 62a**.

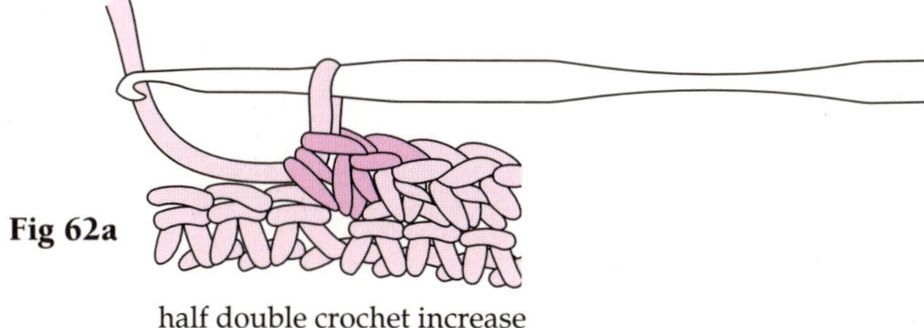

Fig 62a

half double crochet increase

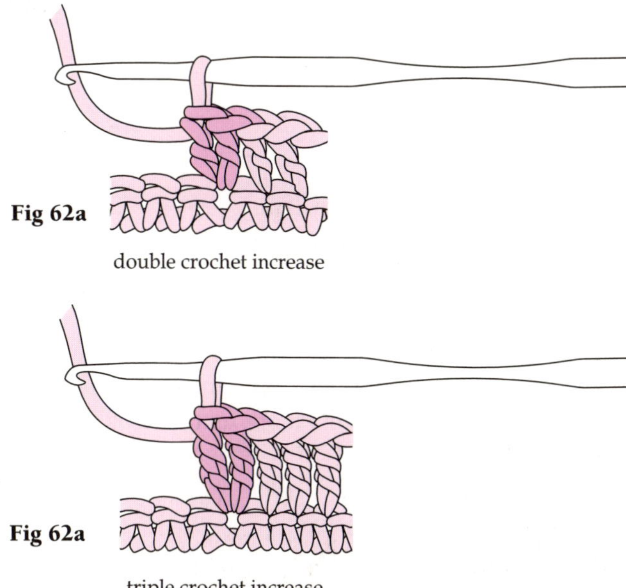

Fig 62a

double crochet increase

Fig 62a

triple crochet increase

Note: Make another practice sample by chaining 15 loosely and working 4 rows of single crochet. Do not finish off at end of last row. Use this sample swatch to practice the following methods of decreasing stitches.

Decreasing: This is how to work a decrease in the four main stitches. Each decrease gives one fewer stitch than you had before.

Single Crochet Decrease: Insert hook and draw up a loop in each of the next 2 stitches (3 loops now on hook), hook thread and draw through all 3 loops on the hook (**Fig 63**).

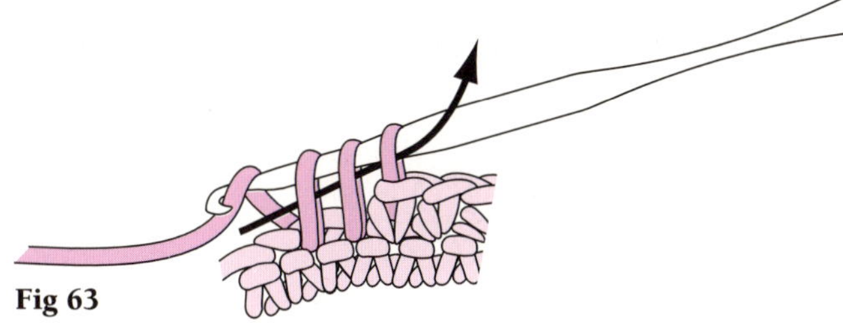

Fig 63

Single crochet decrease made (**Fig 64**).

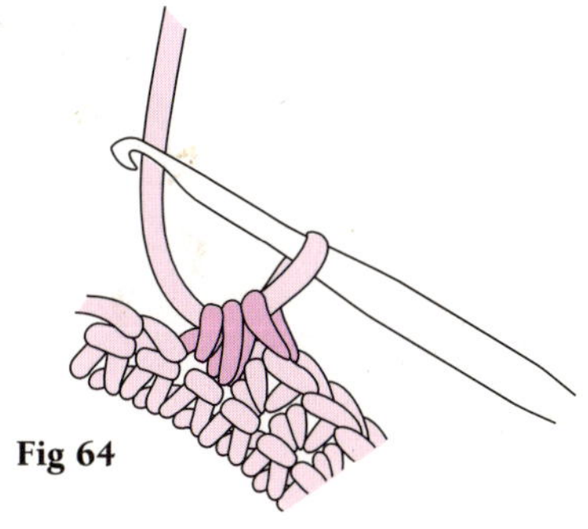

Fig 64

Double Crochet Decrease: Work a double crochet in the specified stitch until 2 loops remain on the hook (**Fig 65**).

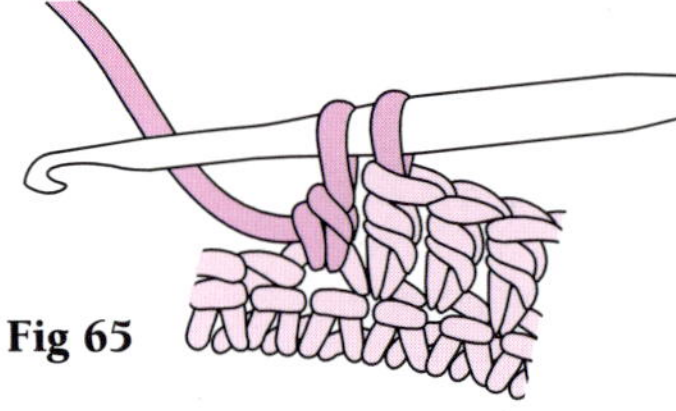
Fig 65

Keeping these 2 loops on hook, work another double crochet in the next stitch until 3 loops remain on hook; hook thread and draw through all 3 loops on the hook (**Fig 66**).

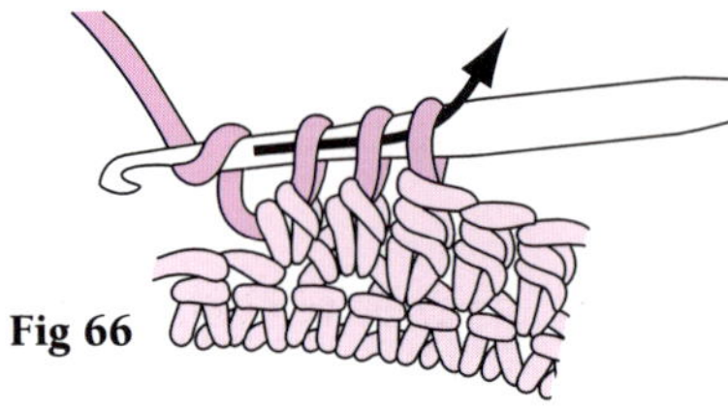
Fig 66

Double crochet decrease made (**Fig 67**).

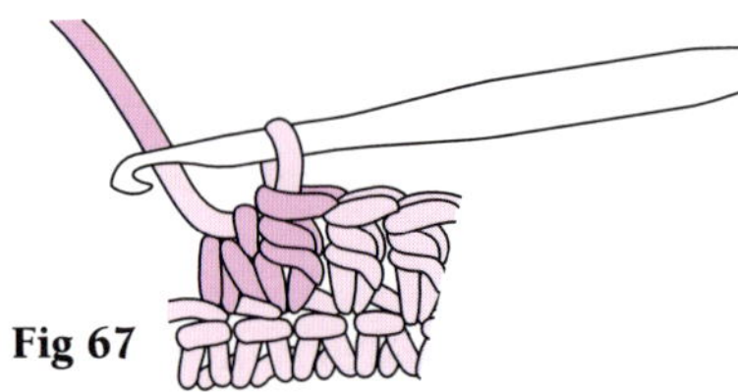
Fig 67

Half Double Crochet Decrease: YO, insert hook in specified stitch and draw up a loop: 3 loops on the hook (**Fig 68**).

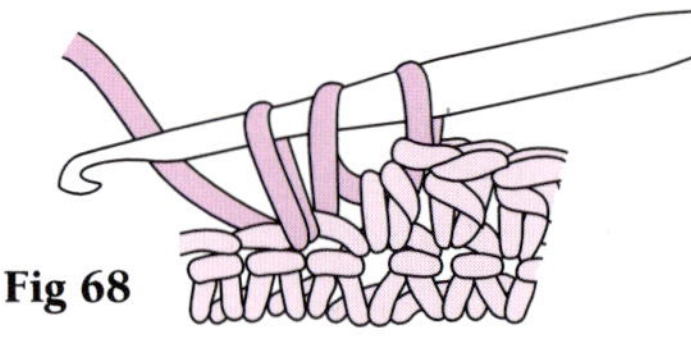
Fig 68

Keeping these 3 loops on hook, YO and draw up a loop in the next stitch (5 loops now on hook), hook thread and draw through all 5 loops on the hook (**Fig 69**).

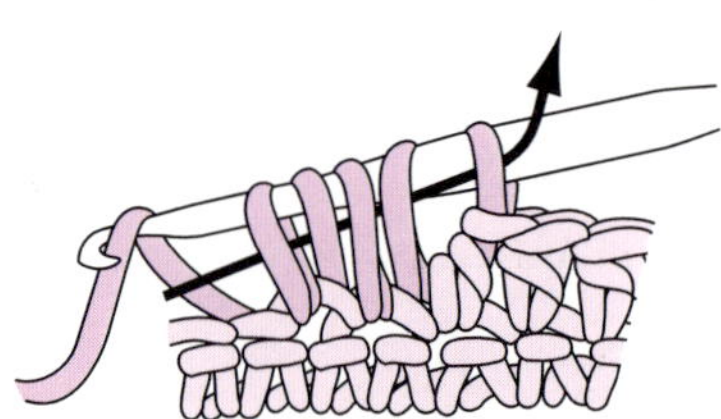
Fig 69

Half double crochet decrease made (**Fig 70**).

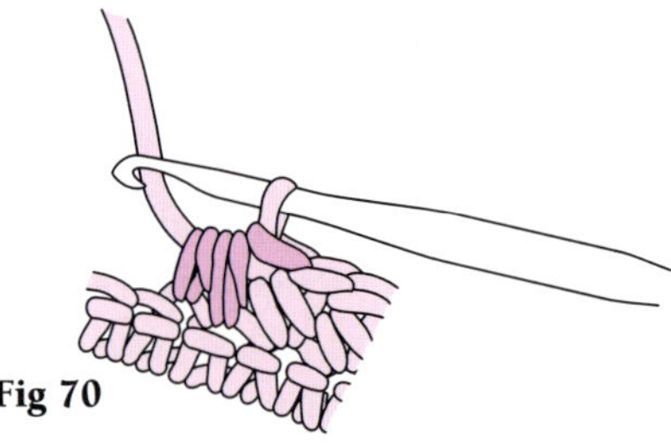
Fig 70

Triple Crochet Decrease: Work a triple crochet in the specified stitch until 2 loops remain on the hook (**Fig 71**).

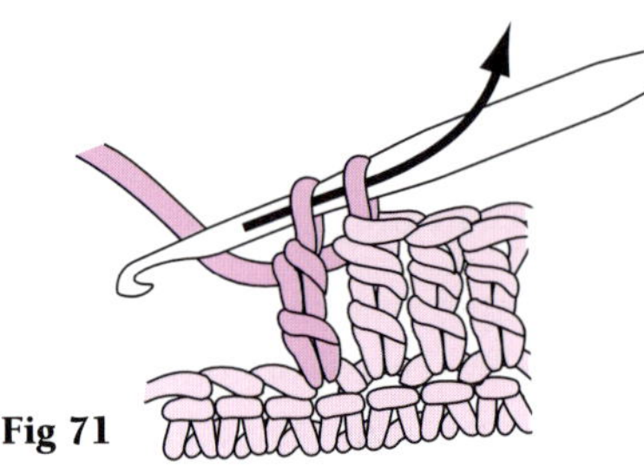
Fig 71

Keeping these 2 loops on hook, work another triple crochet in the next stitch until 3 loops remain on the hook, hook thread and draw through all 3 loops on the hook (**Fig 72**).

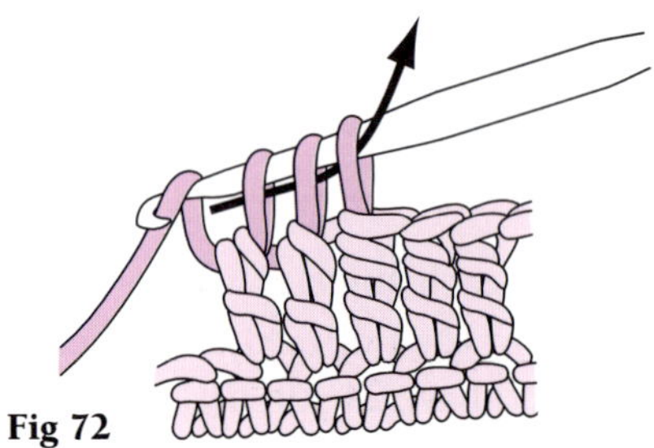
Fig 72

Triple crochet decrease made (**Fig 73**).

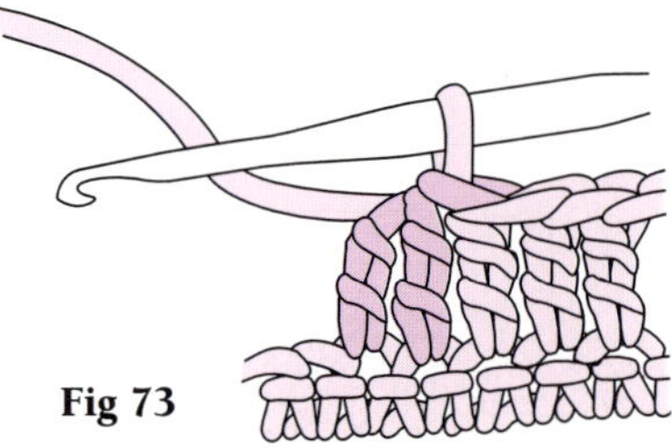
Fig 73

Joining New Thread

Never tie or leave knots! In crochet, thread ends can be easily worked in and hidden because of the density of the stitches. Always leave at least 4" ends when finishing off thread just used and when joining new thread. If a flaw or a knot appears in the thread while you are working from a ball, cut out the imperfection and rejoin the thread.

Whenever possible, join new thread at the end of a row. To do this, work the last stitch with the old thread until 2 loops remain on the hook, then with the new thread complete the stitch (**Fig 74**).

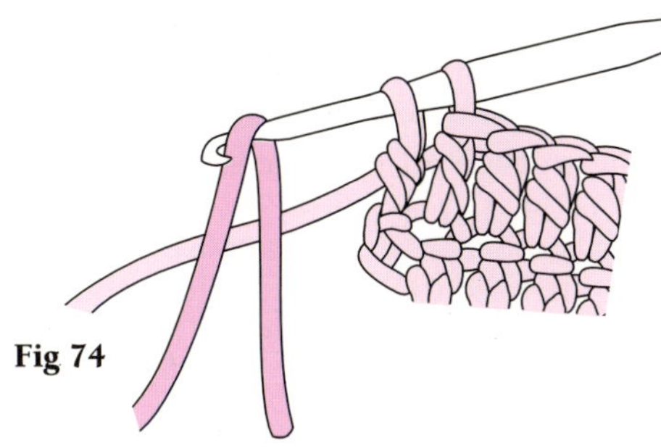

Fig 74

To join new thread in the middle of a row, when about 8" of the old thread remain, work several more stitches with the old thread, working the stitches over the end of new thread (**Fig 75** shown in double crochet). Then change threads in stitch as previously explained.

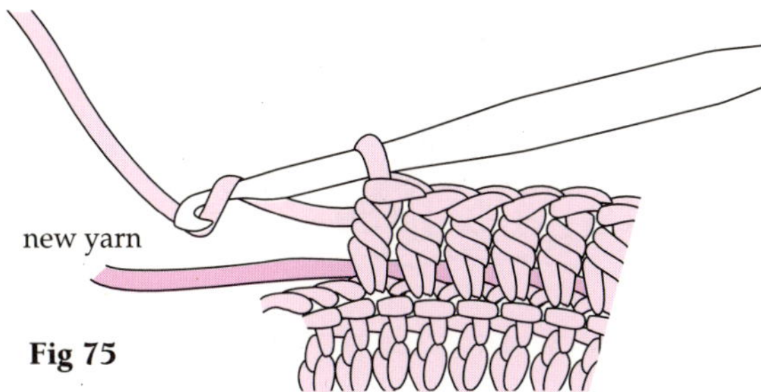

Fig 75

Continuing with the new thread, work the following stitches over the old thread end.

Finishing

A carefully crocheted project can be disappointing if the finishing has been done incorrectly. Correct finishing techniques are not difficult, but do require time, attention, and a knowledge of basic techniques.

Weaving in Ends: After completing your project, it is necessary to securely weave in all thread ends. Thread a size 18 steel tapestry needle with thread, then weave running stitches either horizontally or vertically on the wrong side of work. First weave about 1" in one direction and then 1/2" in the reverse direction. Be sure thread doesn't show on right side of work. Cut off excess thread. Never weave in more than one thread end at a time.

Starching and Blocking

Starching Supplies

Some thread crochet projects have a more finished look when starched. The following supplies will be necessary to starch the snowflake projects on pages 25 through 27.

1. Stiffening solution. Use one of the following:

(a) Equal amounts of water and commercial stiffening solution (available in your local craft or needlework store), thoroughly mixed.

(b) Equal amounts of white craft glue and water, thoroughly mixed.

(c) Thick solution of commercial boilable starch (liquid or spray starches won't do the job).

2. Plastic bag. Use a plastic bag that locks across the top for mixing solution and soaking snowflakes.

3. Pinning board. Use a sheet of Styrofoam® (our preference), a piece of corrugated cardboard, or a fabric cutting board.

4. Plastic wrap. Cover pinning board with plastic wrap so snowflakes can be easily removed.

5. Rust-proof pins. Use pins to hold edges of snowflakes in place while drying.

Starching Instructions

Step 1. Wash your finished project carefully by hand using a mild soap. Rinse well in warm water.

Step 2. Pour prepared stiffening solution into plastic bag and place in a bowl. Immerse snowflakes in solution and let soak one minute. Remove and press out extra solution. Do not squeeze - snowflakes should be very wet, but there should be no solution in the decorative holes (dab with a dry paper towel to correct this). Any excess stiffening solution can be stored in the locked plastic bag for as long as one week, mixing before each use.

Step 3. Place project on pinning board or large piece of styrofoam®. Pin to shape, using rust-proof pins. Let dry.

Blocking Instructions

To block a project, follow Steps 1 and 3 of Starching Instructions.

Reading Patterns (abbreviations, symbols and terms)

Crochet patterns are written in a special language full of abbreviations, asterisks, parentheses, and other symbols and terms. These short forms are used so instructions will not take up too much space. They may seem confusing at first, but once understood, they are really easy to follow.

Abbreviations

beg..begin(ning)
bl(s)....................................back loop(s)
ch(s)...chain(s)
CL ....cluster(s)
dc................................double crochet(s)
dec....................................decrease(-ing)
Fig...figure
fl(s)....................................front loop(s)
hdc........................half double crochet(s)
inc....................................increase(-ing)
lp(s)..loop(s)
patt..pattern
PC(s)....................................popcorn(s)
prev...previous
rem......................................remain(ing)
rep..repeat(ing)
rnd(s).......................................round(s)
sc..................................single crochet(s)
sk...skip
sl...slip
sl st(s)..............................slip stitch(es)
sp(s)..space(s)
st(s)..stitch(es)
Tch...................................turning chain
tog..together
trc.................................triple crochet(s)
YO..thread over

Symbols

* An asterisk is used to mark the beginning of a portion of instructions which will be worked more than once; thus, "rep from * twice" means after working the instructions once, repeat the instructions following the asterisk twice more (3 times in all).

† The dagger identifies a portion of instructions that will be repeated again later in the same row or round.

: The number after the colon at the end of a row or round indicates the number of stitches you should have when the row or round has been completed.

( ) Parentheses are used to enclose instructions which should be worked the exact number of times specified immediately following the parentheses, such as: (ch 3, dc) twice. They are also used to set off and clarify a group of stitches that are to be worked all into the same space or stitch, such as: in corner sp work (2 dc, ch 1, 2 dc).

[ ] Brackets and ( ) parentheses are used to provide additional information to clarify instructions.

Terms

Front loop is the loop toward you at the top of the stitch (**Fig 76**).

Back loop is the loop away from you at the top of the stitch (**Fig 76**).

Post is the vertical part of the stitch (**Fig 76**).

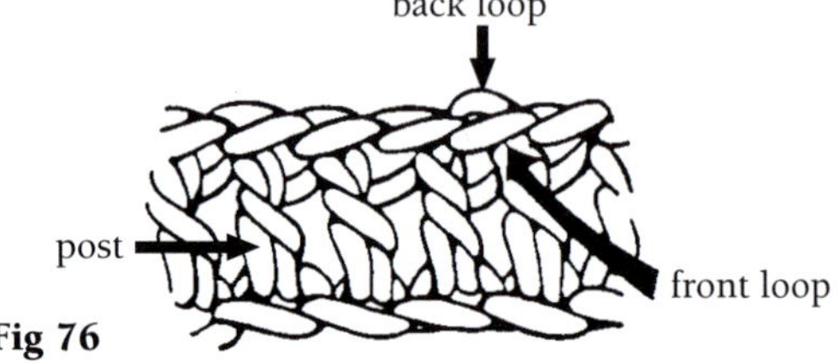

Fig 76

Work even means to continue to work in the pattern as established, without increasing or decreasing.

Wrong Side: Wrong side of the work – the side that will not show when project is in use.

Right Side: The side that will show.

Right-hand Side: The side nearest your right hand as you are working.

Left-hand Side: The side nearest your left hand as you are working.

Right Front: The piece of a garment that will be worn on the right-hand side of the body.

Left Front: The piece of a garment that will be worn on the left-hand side of the body.

Gauge

We've left this until last, but it really is the single most important thing in crochet.

If you don't work to gauge, your crocheted projects may not be the correct size, and you may not have enough thread to finish your project.

Gauge means the number of stitches per inch and rows per inch, that result from a specified thread worked with a specified size hook. Since everyone crochets differently – some loosely, some tightly, some in between – the measurements of individual work can vary greatly when using the same size hook and thread. It is **your responsibility** to make sure you achieve the gauge specified in the pattern.

Hook sizes given in instructions are merely guides and should never be used without making a 4" square sample swatch to check gauge. Make the sample gauge swatch using the size hook and the thread and stitch specified in the pattern. If you have more stitches per inch than specified, try again using a larger size hook. If you have fewer stitches per inch than specified, try again using a smaller size hook. Do not hesitate to change to a larger or smaller size hook if necessary to achieve gauge.

If you have the correct number of stitches per inch, but cannot achieve the row gauge, adjust the height of your stitches. This means that after inserting the hook to begin a new stitch, draw up a little more thread if your stitches are not tall enough – this makes the first loop slightly higher; or draw up less thread if your stitches are too tall. Practice will help you achieve the correct height.

Photo G shows how to measure your gauge.

Photo G

Metric Conversion Charts

INCHES INTO MILLIMETERS & CENTIMETERS *(Rounded off slightly)*

inches	mm	cm	inches	cm	inches	cm	inches	cm
1/8	3		5	12.5	21	53.5	38	96.5
1/4	6		5 1/2	14	22	56	39	99
3/8	10	1	6	15	23	58.5	40	101.5
1/2	13	1.3	7	18	24	61	41	104
5/8	15	1.5	8	20.5	25	63.5	42	106.5
3/4	20	2	9	23	26	66	43	109
7/8	22	2.2	10	25.5	27	68.5	44	112
1	25	2.5	11	28	28	71	45	114.5
1 1/4	32	3.2	12	30.5	29	73.5	46	117
1 1/2	38	3.8	13	33	30	76	47	119.5
1 3/4	45	4.5	14	35.5	31	79	48	122
2	50	5	15	38	32	81.5	49	124.5
2 1/2	65	6.5	16	40.5	33	84	50	127
3	75	7.5	17	43	34	86.5		
3 1/2	90	9	18	46	35	89		
4	100	10	19	48.5	36	91.5		
4 1/2	115	11.5	20	51	37	94		

mm – millimeter cm – centimeter

CROCHET HOOKS CONVERSION CHART

U.S.	1	2	3	4	5	6	7	8	9	10	11	12	13	14
English	3/0	2/0	1/0	1	1 1/2	2	2 1/2	3	4	5	5 1/2	6	6 1/2	7
Continental-mm	3	2.5		2		1.75	1.5	1.25	1	0.75		0.6		

Shell Edging

Size:

Worked to desired length

Materials:

Bedspread-weight crochet cotton, one 225-yd ball white
Size 7 steel crochet hook, or size required for gauge

Gauge:

9 dc = 1"

Instructions

Ch 16.

Row 1: 2 dc in 4th ch from hook (3 skipped chs count as a dc), ch 2, 3 dc in same ch: beg shell made; * sk next 2 chs, sc in next ch, sk next 2 chs, in next ch work (3 dc, ch 2, 3 dc): shell made; rep from * once more; ch 3, turn.

Row 2: * Shell in ch-2 sp of next shell; rep from * twice more; ch 3, turn.

Rep Row 2 until desired length. At end of last row, do not ch 3. Finish off and weave in ends.

Scalloped Edging

Size:

Fits 16" hand towel

Materials:

Bedspread-weight crochet cotton, one 225-yd ball white
Size 7 steel crochet hook, or size required for gauge

Gauge:

9 dc = 1"

Instructions

Foundation:

Ch 8.

Row 1: Dc in 6th ch from hook (5 skipped chs count as a ch-1 sp, a dc, and a ch-1 sp); ch 1, sk next ch, dc in next ch; ch 4 (counts as first dc and ch-1 sp on following rows), turn.

Row 2: Dc in next dc, ch 1, sk next ch-1 sp, dc in next dc, ch 1, dc in next dc (2nd ch of 5 skipped chs at beg of Row 1); ch 4, turn.

Row 3: Dc in next dc, ch 1, sk next ch-1 sp, dc in next dc, ch 1, sk next ch-1 sp, dc in next dc (2nd ch of turning ch-4); ch 4, turn.

Rows 4 through 43: Rep Row 3. At end of Row 43, do not ch 4; ch 1, turn so long edge is at top.

Border:

Row 1 (right side)**:** Sl st in next lp; ch 1, working in lps made by end sts, sc in next lp, * ch 4, sc in next lp; rep from * across; ch 1, turn.

Row 2: Sl st in next ch-4 lp; ch 1, sc in same lp; in next ch-4 lp work (3 dc, ch 2, 3 dc): shell made; sc in next ch-4 lp, * ch 4, sc in next ch-4 lp, in next ch-4 lp work (3 dc, ch 2, 3 dc): shell made; sc in next ch-4 lp; rep from * across; ch 4, turn.

Row 3: In ch-2 sp of next shell work (dc, ch 1, dc, ch 1, dc); * ch 2, sc in next ch-4 lp, ch 2, in ch-2 sp of next shell work (dc, ch 1, dc, ch 1, dc); rep from * across; ch 4, sc in next sc; ch 1, turn.

Row 4: Sl st in next ch-4 lp; ch 1, sc in same lp; (ch 4, sc in next ch-1 sp) twice; * ch 4, sc in next ch-2 sp, in next sc, and in next ch-2 sp; (ch 4, sc in next ch-1 sp) twice; rep from * across; ch 4, sc in next ch-4 lp. Finish off and weave in ends.

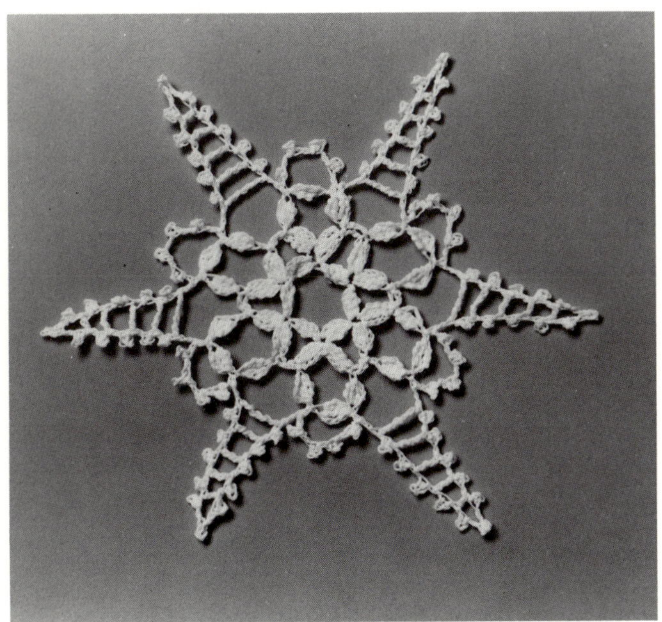

Crystal Snowflake

Size:

About 6" x 6"

Materials:

Bedspread-weight crochet cotton, 100 yds white
Size 7 steel crochet hook, or size required for gauge
Starching and blocking supplies (see page 20)

Gauge:

9 sc = 1"

Pattern Stitches:

Double Triple Crochet (dtrc):
YO 3 times, draw up lp in next st, (YO, draw through 2 lps on hook) 4 times: dtrc made.

Triple Triple Crochet (trtrc):
YO 4 times, draw up lp in next st, (YO, draw through 2 lps on hook) 5 times: trtrc made.

Beginning Cluster (beg CL):
Ch 4, keeping last lp of each st on hook, 2 trc in same st as joining; YO and draw through all 3 lps on hook: beg CL made.

Cluster (CL):
Keeping last lp of each st on hook, 3 trc in next st, YO and draw through all 4 lps on hook: CL made.

Instructions

Rnd 1: * Ch 5, CL (see Pattern Stitches) in 4th ch from hook; rep from * 5 times more; join in first ch to form a ring: 6 CLs.

Rnd 2: Beg CL (see Pattern Stitches) in same ch as joining; ch 4, in same ch work (sl st, ch 4, CL); * ch 3, in ch between next 2 CL work (CL, ch 4, sl st, ch 4, CL); rep from * 4 times more; ch 3; join in top of beg CL.

Rnd 3: * (Ch 5, CL in 4th ch from hook) 3 times; sl st in top of next CL, ch 3, sl st in top of next CL; rep from * 5 times more, ending last rep without working last sl st; join in first ch of beg ch-5.

Rnd 4: Sl st in next 4 chs of same beg ch-5 of Rnd 3 and in top of next CL; * sc in ch between CLs, (ch 5, sl st in 4th ch from hook: picot made) 4 times; ch 1, sc in ch between next 2 CLs; ch 6, sl st in 4th ch from hook: picot made; (ch 5, sl st in 4th ch from hook: picot made) 6 times; sk next 2 picots, dc in ch between next 2 picots; ch 4, sl st in 4th ch from hook: picot made; trc in ch between next 2 picots; ch 4, sl st in 4th ch from hook: picot made; trc in ch between next 2 picots; ch 4, sl st in 4th ch from hook: picot made; dtrc (see Pattern Stitches) in ch between next 2 picots; ch 4, sl st in 4th ch from hook: picot made; trtrc (see Pattern Stitches) in ch after next picot; ch 2, sk next CL, next ch-3 lp, and next CL; rep from * 5 times more; join in beg sc.

Finish off and weave in ends.

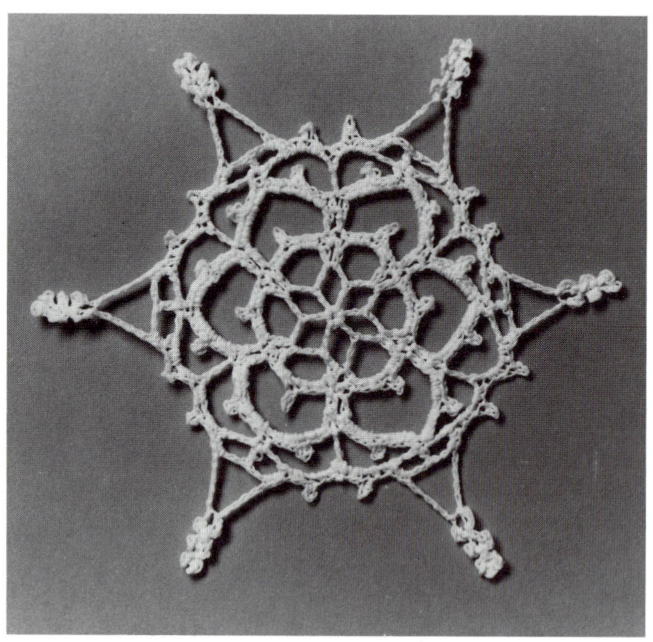

Suzy Snowflake

Size:

About 6" x 6"

Materials:

Bedspread-weight crochet cotton, 100 yds white
Size 7 steel crochet hook, or size required for gauge
Starching and blocking supplies (see page 0)

Gauge:

9 sc = 1"

Instructions

Ch 4, join to form a ring.

Rnd 1: Ch 8 (counts as a dc and a ch-5 lp), dc in ring, (ch 5, dc in ring) 4 times; ch 5; join in 3rd ch of beg ch-8: 6 ch-5 lps.

Rnd 2: Sl st in next lp; ch 1, in same lp work (sc, ch 3, sc); ch 7, * in next lp work (sc, ch 3, sc); ch 7; rep from * around; join in first sc.

Rnd 3: Sl st in next ch-3 lp; ch 1, 2 sc in same lp; * in next ch-7 lp work (3 sc; ch 4, sl st in 4th ch from hook: picot made; 3 sc); 2 sc in next ch-3 lp; rep from * around, ending last rep without working last 2 sc; join in first sc.

Rnd 4: Ch 1, sc in same sc as joining; * ch 3, sc in next sc, ch 15, sk next 3 sc, next picot, and next 3 sc; sc in next sc; rep from * around, ending last rep without working last sc; join in first sc.

Rnd 5: Sl st in next ch-3 lp; ch 1, * sc in same lp; in next ch-15 lp work (4 sc, picot) 3 times; 4 sc in same lp; sc in next lp; rep from * around, ending last rep without working last sc; join in first sc.

Rnd 6: Ch 8, sk next picot, in next picot work (dc, ch 5, dc, ch 5, dc); ch 5, sk next picot and next 4 sc, * dc in next sc, ch 5, sk next picot, in next picot work (dc, ch 5, dc, ch 5, dc); ch 5, sk next picot; rep from * around; join in 3rd ch of beg ch-8.

Rnd 7: Sl st in next ch-5 lp; ch 1, in same lp work (2 sc, picot, 2 sc); * 2 sc in next ch-5 lp; ch 5, picot twice; ch 4, in 4th ch from hook work (sl st, ch 3, sl st, ch 3, sl st); † in ch at base of next picot work (sl st, ch 3, sl st) †; rep from † to † once more; ch 5, 2 sc in next ch-5 lp; in each of next 2 ch-5 lps work (2 sc, picot, 2 sc); rep from * around, ending last rep without working last (2 sc, picot, 2 sc); join in first sc. Finish off and weave in ends.

Frosted Flake

Size:

About 6" x 6"

Materials:

Bedspread-weight crochet cotton, 100 yds white
Size 7 steel crochet hook, or size required for gauge
Starching and blocking supplies (see page 20)

Gauge:

9 sc = 1"

Pattern Stitches

Double Triple Crochet (dtrc):
YO 3 times, draw up lp in next st, (YO, draw through 2 lps on hook) 4 times: dtrc made.

Cluster (CL):
Keeping last lp of each trc on hook, 3 trc in next st, YO and draw through all 4 lps on hook: CL made.

Instructions

Ch 5, join to form a ring.

Rnd 1: Ch 7 (counts as a dc and a ch-4 lp), dc in ring; (ch 4, dc in ring) 4 times; ch 4; join in 3rd ch of beg ch-7: 6 ch-4 lps.

Rnd 2: Sl st in next ch-4 lp; ch 1, 6 sc in same lp and in each rem ch-4 lp; join in first sc.

Rnd 3: Ch 1, sc in same sc as joining; [ch 5, CL (see Pattern Stitches) in 5th ch from hook] twice; * sk next 5 sc, sc in next sc, (ch 5, CL in 5th ch from hook) twice; rep from * 5 times more; sk next 5 sc; join in first sc.

Rnd 4: Ch 9 (counts as a trc and a ch-5 lp), * CL in 5th ch from hook; ch 2, trc in sp between next 2 CLs; ch 4, sl st in 4th ch from hook: picot made; picot as before 3 times more; ch 3, picot as before 4 times; sl st in last trc made; ch 7, CL in 5th ch from hook; trc in sc between next 2 CLs, ch 5; rep from * 5 times more, ending last rep without working last trc and last ch-5; join in 4th ch of beg ch-4.

Rnd 5: Ch 8 (counts as a dtrc and a ch-3 lp), dtrc (see Pattern Stitches) in same ch as joining; ch 7, 5 dc in ch-3 lp (at tip of point); ch 7, * in next trc work (dtrc, ch 3, dtrc); ch 7, 5 dc in ch-3 lp (at tip of next point); ch 7, rep from * around; join in 5th ch of beg ch-8.

Rnd 6: Sl st in next ch-3 lp; ch 1, in same lp work (2 sc, picot, 2 sc); 7 sc in next ch-7 lp; * † in next dc work (sl st, ch 4, dtrc); ch 5, sl st in dtrc just made: ch-5 picot made; ch 4, sl st in same dc as last dtrc made †; rep from † to † in each of next 4 dc; 7 sc in next ch-7 lp; in next lp work (2 sc, picot, 2 sc); 7 sc in next ch-7 lp; rep from * around; join in first sc. Finish off and weave in ends.

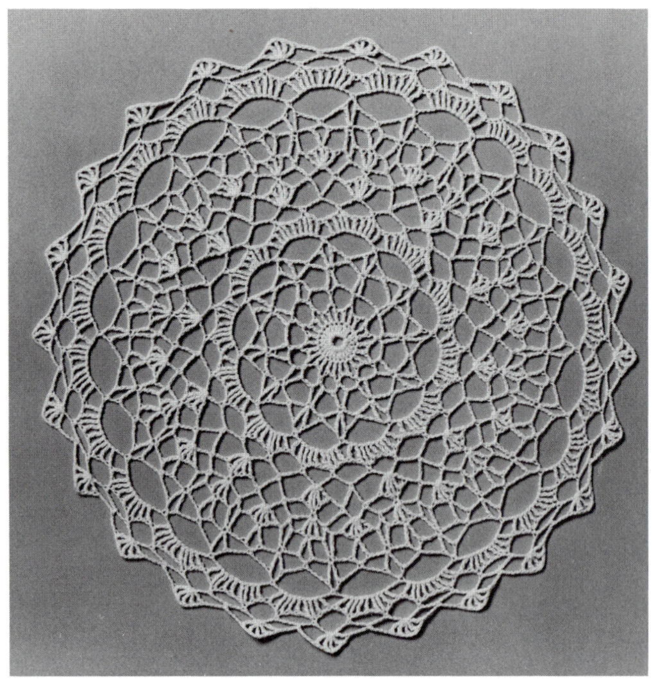

Simplicity Doily

Size:
About 11 1/2" diameter

Materials:
Bedspread-weight crochet cotton, one 225-yd ball cream
Size 7 steel crochet hook, or size required for gauge

Gauge:
9 dc = 1"

Instructions

Ch 8, join to form a ring.

Rnd 1: Ch 3 (counts as a dc on this and following rnds), 23 dc in ring; join in 3rd ch of beg ch-3: 24 dc.

Rnd 2: Ch 6 (counts as a dc and a ch-3 lp), dc in next dc, ch 1, * dc in next dc, ch 3, dc in next dc, ch 1; rep from * around; join in 3rd ch of beg ch-6: 12 ch-3 lps.

Rnd 3: Sl st in next ch-3 lp; ch 9 (counts as a dc and a ch-6 lp), * dc in next ch-3 lp, ch 6; rep from * around; join in 3rd ch of beg ch-9.

Rnd 4: Sl st in next ch-6 lp; ch 12 (counts as a trc and a ch-8 lp); * keeping last lp of each trc on hook, trc in same ch-6 lp and in next ch-6 lp, YO and draw through all 3 lps on hook: cluster made; ch 8; rep from * around; join in 3rd ch of beg ch-12: 12 ch-8 lps.

Rnd 5: Ch 7 (counts as a trc and a ch-3 lp), trc in same ch as joining; ch 3, sc in next ch-8 lp, ch 3, * in top of next cluster work (trc, ch 3, trc); ch 3, sc in next ch-8 lp, ch 3; rep from * around; join in 4th ch of beg ch-7.

Rnd 6: Sl st in next ch-3 lp; ch 1, sc in same lp; ch 11, sk next 2 ch-3 lps, * sc in next ch-3 lp, ch 11, sk next 2 ch-3 lps; rep from * around; join in first sc.

Rnd 7: Ch 1, sk first ch of next ch-11 lp, sl st in next ch; ch 5 (counts as a trc and a ch-1 sp), trc in next ch, (ch 1, trc in next ch) 7 times; sk next ch, * sk first ch of next ch-11 lp, trc in next ch, (ch 1, trc in next ch) 8 times; sk next ch; rep from * around; join in 4th ch of beg ch-5.

Rnd 8: Ch 1, sl st in next ch, in next trc, in next ch, and in next trc; ch 1, sc in same trc as last sl st made; ch 7, * sk next 3 trc, sc in next trc, ch 7, sk next 4 trc, sc in next trc, ch 7; rep from * around; join in first sc.

Rnd 9: Sl st in next 4 chs of next ch-7 lp; ch 5, in same ch as last sl st made work [trc, (ch 1, trc) 3 times]; ch 7, sc in next ch-7 lp, ch 7, * trc in 4th ch of next ch-7 lp, in same ch work (ch 1, trc) 4 times; ch 7, sc in next ch-7 lp, ch 7; rep from * around; join in 4th ch of beg ch-5.

Rnd 10: Sl st in next ch, in next trc, in next ch, and in next trc; ch 1, sc in same trc as last sl st made; ch 7, (sc in next ch-7 lp, ch 7) twice; * sc in 3rd trc of next 5-trc group, ch 7, (sc in next ch-7 lp, ch 7) twice; rep from * around; join in first sc.

Rnd 11: Ch 5, in same sc work (trc, ch 1, trc); * † ch 3, sc in next ch-7 lp, ch 3, in 4th ch of next ch-7 lp work (trc, ch 1) 4 times; trc in same ch; ch 3, sc in next ch-7 lp, ch 3 †, in next sc work (trc, ch 1) twice; trc in same sc; rep from * 10 times more, then rep from † to † once; join in 4th ch of beg ch-5.

Rnd 12: Sl st in next ch and in next trc; ch 7, trc in same trc; * ch 3, keeping last lp of each trc on hook, trc in each of next 2 ch-3 lps, YO and draw through all 3 lps on hook: cluster made; ch 3, in 3rd trc of next 5-trc group work (trc, ch 3, trc); ch 3, keeping last lp of each trc on hook, trc in each of next 2 ch-3 lps, YO and draw through all 3 lps on hook: cluster made; ch 3, in 2nd trc of next 3-trc group work (trc, ch 3, trc); rep from * around, ending last rep without working last (trc, ch 3, trc); join in 4th ch of beg ch-7.

Rnd 13: Sl st in next ch-3 lp; ch 1, sc in same lp; * ch 4, sk next ch-3 lp, in top of next cluster work (trc, ch 3, trc);

Allexown - RAE 378

ch 4, sk next ch-3 lp, sc in next ch-3 lp; rep from * around, ending last rep without working last sc; join in first sc.

Rnd 14: Sl st in next 4 chs, in next trc, and in next ch-3 lp; ch 1, sc in same lp; * ch 13, sk next 2 ch-4 lps, sc in next ch-3 lp; rep from * around, ending last rep without working last sc; join in first sc: 24 ch-13 lps.

Rnd 15: Sl st in next 3 chs of next ch-13 lp; ch 5, trc in next ch, (ch 1, trc in next ch) 7 times; sk next 2 chs; * sk next 2 chs of next ch-13 lp, trc in next ch, (ch 1, trc in next ch) 8 times; sk next 2 chs; rep from * around; join in 4th ch of beg ch-5.

Rnd 16: Rep Rnd 8.

Rnd 17: Sl st in next 4 chs of next ch-7 lp; ch 1, sc in same ch as last sl st made; * ch 4, trc in 4th ch of next ch-7 lp; in same lp work (ch 1, trc) 4 times; ch 4, sc in next ch-7 lp; rep from * around, ending last rep without working last sc; join in first sc. Finish off and weave in ends.

Lacy Bouquet Doily

Size:

About 11" diameter

Materials:

Bedspread-weight crochet cotton, one 225-yd ball cream
Size 7 steel crochet hook, or size required for gauge

Gauge:

9 dc = 1"

Instructions

Ch 5, join to form a ring.

Rnd 1: Ch 5 (counts as a dc and a ch-2 sp), dc in ring; ch 2, (dc in ring, ch 2) 6 times; join in 3rd ch of beg ch-5: 8 ch-2 sps.

Rnd 2: Sl st in next ch-2 sp; ch 3 (counts as a dc on this and following rnds), 2 dc in same sp; ch 1, * 3 dc in next ch-2 sp; ch 1; rep from * around; join in 3rd ch of beg ch-3.

Rnd 3: Ch 3, dc in next 2 dc, ch 4, sk next ch-1 sp, * dc in next 3 dc, ch 4, sk next ch-1 sp; rep from * around; join in 3rd ch of beg ch-3.

Rnd 4: Sl st in next 2 dc and in next ch-4 lp; ch 3, in same lp work (dc, ch 3, 2 dc); ch 5, * in next ch-4 lp work (2 dc, ch 3, 2 dc); ch 5; rep from * around; join in 3rd ch of beg ch-3.

Rnd 5: Sl st in next dc and in next ch-3 lp; ch 3, in same lp work (2 dc, ch 3, 3 dc): beg shell made; * ch 5, sk next ch-5 lp, in next ch-3 lp work (3 dc, ch 3, 3 dc): shell made; rep from * to last ch-5 lp; sk next ch-5 lp; join in 3rd ch of beg ch-3.

Rnd 6: Sl st in next 2 dc and in next ch-3 lp; beg shell in same lp; * ch 5, sc in next ch-5 lp in 2nd rnd below (over both ch-5 lps), ch 5, in ch-3 lp of next shell work shell: shell in shell made; rep from * around, ending last rep without working last shell; join in 3rd ch of beg ch-3.

Rnd 7: Sl st in next 2 dc and in next ch-3 lp; beg shell in same lp; * ch 3, sc in next ch-5 lp, ch 5, sc in next ch-5 lp, ch 3, shell in next shell; rep from * around, ending last rep without working last shell; join in 3rd ch of beg ch-3.

Rnd 8: Sl st in next 2 dc and in next ch-3 lp; beg shell in same lp; * ch 5, sk next ch-3 lp, in next ch-5 lp work (2 trc, ch 3, 2 trc); ch 5, sk next ch-3 lp, shell in next shell; rep from * around, ending last rep without working last shell; join in 3rd ch of beg ch-3.

Rnd 9: Sl st in next 2 dc and in next ch-3 lp; beg shell in same lp; * ch 5, sk next ch-5 lp, shell in next ch-3 lp; ch 5, sk next ch-5 lp, shell in next shell; rep from * around, ending last rep without working last shell; join in 3rd ch of beg ch-3.

Rnd 10: Sl st in next 2 dc and in next ch-3 lp; beg shell in same lp; * ch 4, sl st in 4th ch from hook: picot made; ch 4, sc in next ch-5 lp in 2nd rnd below; ch 8, sl st in 4th ch from hook: picot made; shell in next shell; rep from * around, ending last rep without working last shell; join in 3rd ch of beg ch-3.

Rnd 11: Sl st in next 2 dc and in next ch-3 lp; ch 1, sc in same lp; * ch 4, sc in next picot, ch 4, sk next 2 ch-4 lps, sc in next picot; ch 4, sc in ch-3 lp of next shell; rep from * around, ending last rep without working last sc; join in first sc.

Rnd 12: Ch 3, 3 dc in next ch-4 lp; * dc in next sc, 3 dc in next ch-4 lp; rep from * around; join in 3rd ch of beg ch-3.

Rnd 13: Sl st in next dc; ch 3, dc in next 6 dc, ch 3, sk next dc, * dc in next 7 dc, ch 3, sk next dc; rep from * around; join in 3rd ch of beg ch-3.

Rnd 14: Sl st in next 6 dc and in next ch-3 lp; ch 7 (counts as a trc and a ch-3 lp), trc in same lp; * ch 4, sk next 3 dc, sc in next dc, ch 4, sk next 3 dc, in next ch-3 lp work (trc, ch 3, trc); rep from * 22 times more; ch 4, sk next 3 sl sts, sc in next sl st, ch 4; join in 4th ch of beg ch-7.

Rnd 15: Sl st in next ch-3 lp; ch 3, in same lp work (dc, ch 3, 2 dc); * ch 7, sk next 2 ch-4 lps, in next ch-3 lp work (2 dc, ch 3, 2 dc); rep from * 22 times more; ch 7; join in 3rd ch of beg ch-3.

Rnd 16: Sl st in next dc and in next ch-3 lp; beg shell in same lp; ch 7, sk next ch-7 lp, * shell in next shell; ch 7, sk next ch-7 lp; rep from * around; join in 3rd ch of beg ch-3.

Rnd 17: Sl st in next 2 dc and in next ch-3 lp; beg shell in same lp; ch 8, sk next ch-7 lp; * shell in next shell; ch 8, sk next ch-7 lp; rep from * around; join in 3rd ch of beg ch-3.

Rnd 18: Sl st in next 2 dc and in next ch-3 lp; ch 6, hdc in 3rd ch from hook: hdc picot made; dc in ch-3 lp of same shell, † ch 3, hdc in top of dc just made: hdc picot made; dc in same lp †; rep from † to † twice more; * ch 6, sc in next ch-7 lp in 3rd rnd below (over 3 lps), ch 6, dc in ch-3 lp of next shell; rep from † to † 4 times; rep from * 22 times more; ch 6, sc in next ch-7 lp in 3rd rnd below; ch 6, join in 3rd ch of beg ch-3 (next to hdc picot). Finish off and weave in ends.

Pineapple Tablecloth

Sizes:

Small: 54" x 54" (9 motifs x 9 motifs)
Large: 54" x 72" (9 motifs x 12 motifs)

Note: *To change sizes, simply add or subtract motifs for desired measurements, and remember to adjust the thread amounts accordingly (approx 225 yds of thread are required to work 3 motifs).*

Materials:

Bedspread-weight crochet cotton, 74 yds white per motif (see Sizes)
Size 7 steel crochet hook, or size required for gauge
Size 18 tapestry needle

Gauge:

one motif = 6" square

Instructions

Motif (make 81 motifs for small size, 108 motifs for large size)
With 2 strands held tog, ch 6, join to form a ring.

Rnd 1 (right side)**:** Ch 3 (counts as a dc on this and following rnds), dc in ring, ch 1, (2 dc in ring, ch 1) 7 times; join in 3rd ch of beg ch-3: eight 2-dc groups.

Rnd 2: Ch 3, dc in next dc, * ch 3, sk next ch-1 sp, dc in next 2 dc; rep from * 6 times more; ch 3; join in 3rd ch of beg ch-3.

Rnd 3: Ch 3, dc in next dc, * in next ch-3 lp work (2 dc, ch 3, 2 dc); dc in next 2 dc; rep from * 7 times more, ending last rep without working last 2 dc; join in 3rd ch of beg ch-3.

Rnd 4: Ch 3, dc in next 2 dc, * sk next dc, ch 2, in next ch-3 lp work (dc, ch 3, dc); ch 2, sk next dc, dc in next 4 dc; rep from * 7 times more, ending last rep without working last 3 dc; join in 3rd ch of beg ch-3.

Rnd 5: Ch 3, dc in next dc, * sk next dc, ch 1, sk next ch-2 sp, in next ch-3 lp work (dc, ch 1) 7 times: pineapple base made; sk next ch-2 sp and next dc, dc in next 2 dc; rep from * around, ending last rep without working last 2 dc; join in 3rd ch of beg ch-3: 8 pineapple bases.

Rnd 6: Ch 3, dc in next dc, * ch 1, sk next ch-1 sp, sc in next ch-1 sp, (ch 2, sc in next ch-1 sp) 5 times; ch 1, sk next ch-1 sp, dc in next 2 dc; rep from * around, ending last rep without working last 2 dc; join in 3rd ch of beg ch-3.

Rnd 7: Ch 3, dc in next dc, * ch 2, sk next sp, sc in next ch-2 sp, (ch 2, sc in next ch-2 sp) 4 times; ch 2, sk next sp, dc in next 2 dc; rep from * around, ending last rep without working last 2 dc; join in 3rd ch of beg ch-3.

Rnd 8: Ch 3, dc in same dc as joining; * ch 3: corner lp made; 2 dc in next dc; ch 3, sk next sp, sc in next ch-2 sp, (ch 2, sc in next ch-2 sp) 3 times; ch 3, sk next sp, dc in next 2 dc, ch 3, sk next sp, sc in next ch-2 sp, (ch 2, sc in next ch-2 sp) 3 times; ch 3, sk next sp, 2 dc in next dc; rep from * 3 times more, ending last rep without working last 2 dc; join in 3rd ch of beg ch-3.

Rnd 9: Ch 3, dc in next dc, * in next ch-3 lp work (2 dc, ch 3, 2 dc): corner made; dc in next 2 dc, ch 3, sk next ch-3 lp, sc in next ch-2 sp, (ch 2, sc in next ch-2 sp) twice; ch 3, 2 sc in next ch-3 lp; sc in next 2 dc, 2 sc in next ch-3 lp; ch 3, sc in next ch-2 sp, (ch 2, sc in next ch-2 sp) twice; ch 3, dc in next 2 dc; rep from * 3 times more, ending last rep without working last 2 dc; join in 3rd ch of beg ch-3.

Rnd 10: Ch 3, dc in next 3 dc, * in ch-3 lp of next corner work corner: corner in corner made; dc in next 4 dc, ch 3, sk next ch-3 lp, sc in next ch-2 sp, ch 2, sc in next ch-2 sp, ch 3, 2 sc in next ch-3 lp; sc in next 6 sc, 2 sc in next ch-3 lp; ch 3, sc in next ch-2 sp, ch 2, sc in next ch-2 sp, ch 3, sk next ch-3 lp, dc in next 4 dc; rep from * 3 times more, ending last rep without working last 4 dc; join in 3rd ch of beg ch-3.

Rnd 11: Ch 3, dc in next 5 dc, * corner in next corner; dc in next 6 dc, ch 3, sk next ch-3 lp, sc in next ch-2 sp, ch 3, 2 sc in next ch-3 lp; sc in next 10 sc, 2 sc in next ch-3 lp; ch 3, sc in next ch-2 sp, ch 3, dc in next 6 dc; rep from * 3 times more, ending last rep without working last 6 dc; join in 3rd ch of beg ch-3.

Rnd 12: Ch 3, dc in next dc, * ch 3, sk next 2 dc, dc in next 2 dc, ch 3, sk next 2 dc, corner in next corner; (ch 3, sk next 2 dc, dc in next 2 dc) twice; ch 3, sk next ch-3 lp, 2 dc in next ch-3 lp; (ch 3, sk next 2 sc, dc in next 2 sc) 3 times; ch 3, sk next 2 sc, 2 dc in next ch-3 lp; ch 3, sk next ch-3 lp, dc in next 2 dc; rep from * 3 times more, ending last rep without working last 2 dc; join in 3rd ch of beg ch-3.

Rnd 13: Ch 3, * dc in each dc and 2 dc in each ch-3 lp to next corner; corner in corner; rep from * 3 times more, dc in each dc and 2 dc in each ch-3 lp to beg ch-3; join in 3rd ch of beg ch-3. Finish off, leaving an 18" length for sewing.

Assembling

Join motifs in 9 rows of 9 motifs for small size or 12 rows of 9 motifs for large size. To join motifs, hold 2 motifs with right sides tog. Carefully matching sts on both motifs and with tapestry needle, sew with overcast st in bls only (**Fig 1**) across side, beg and ending with one corner st. Join motifs in rows; then sew rows tog in same manner, being sure that all four-corner junctions are firmly joined.

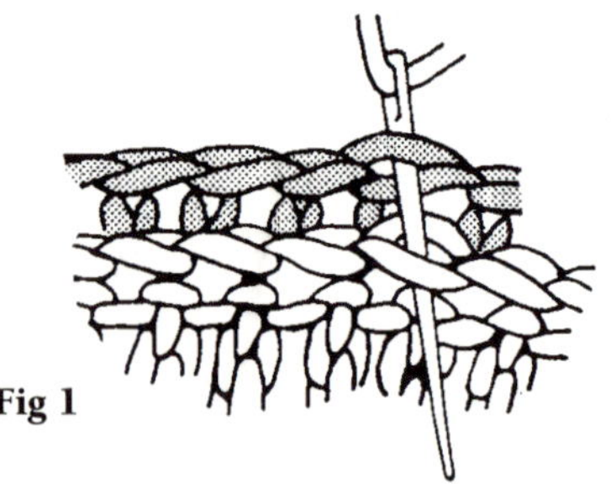

Fig 1

Edging

Hold tablecloth with right side facing you; join thread in any outer corner ch-3 lp; ch 3, in same lp work (2 dc, ch 3, 3 dc): corner made; * † sk next 2 dc, sc in next 2 dc, sk next 2 dc, 3 dc in next dc; ch 3, 3 dc in next dc †; rep from † to † 4 times more; sk next 2 dc, sc in next 2 dc, sk next 2 dc, 3 dc in next corner lp; ch 3, 3 dc in corner lp of next motif; rep from * across to last motif; rep from † to † 5 times; sk next 2 dc, sc in next 2 dc, sk next 2 dc, in next outer corner ch-3 lp work (3 dc, ch 3, 3 dc): corner made; ** †† rep from † to † 5 times; sk next 2 dc, sc in next 2 dc, sk next 2 dc, 3 dc in next corner lp; ch 3, 3 dc in corner lp of next motif ††; rep from †† to †† across to last motif; rep from † to † 5 times; sk next 2 dc, sc in next 2 dc, sk next 2 dc, in next outer corner ch-3 lp work (3 dc, ch 3, 3 dc): corner made; rep from ** twice more, ending last rep without working last corner; join in 3rd ch of beg ch-3.

Finish off and weave in all ends.